THE ISLAMIC DOCTRINE OF CHRISTIANS AND JEWS

BILL WARNER, PHD

CENTER FOR THE STUDY OF
POLITICAL ISLAM

THE ISLAMIC DOCTRINE OF CHRISTIANS AND JEWS

BILL WARNER, PHD

CENTER FOR THE STUDY OF
POLITICAL ISLAM

ISBN13   978-1-936659-00-5

V 09.20.2016

PUBLISHED BY CSPI, LLC
WWW.CSPIPUBLISHING.COM

TABLE OF CONTENTS

This book is dedicated to the
millions of victims of jihad over the last 1400 years.
May you read this and become a voice for the voiceless.

PREFACE

The Center for the Study of Political Islam, CSPI teaching method is the easiest and quickest way to learn about Islam.

Authoritative

There are only two ultimate authorities about Islam—Allah and Mohammed. All of the curriculum in the CSPI method is from the Koran and the Sunna (the words and deeds of Mohammed). The knowledge you get in CSPI is powerful, authoritative and irrefutable. You learn the facts about the ideology of Islam from its ultimate sources.

Story-telling

Facts are hard to remember, stories are easy to remember. The most important story in Islam is the life of Mohammed. Once you know the story of Mohammed, all of Islam is easy to understand.

Systemic Knowledge

The easiest way to study Islam is to first see the whole picture. The perfect example of this is the Koran. The Koran alone cannot be understood, but when the life of Mohammed is added, the Koran is straight forward.

There is no way to understand Islam one idea at the time, because there is no context. Context, like story-telling, makes the facts and ideas simple to understand. The best analogy is that when the jig saw puzzle is assembled, the image on the puzzle is easy to see. But looking at the various pieces, it is difficult to see the picture.

Levels of Learning

The ideas of Islam are very foreign to our civilization. It takes repetition to grasp the new ideas. The CSPI method uses four levels of training to teach the doctrine in depth. The first level is designed for a beginner. Each level repeats the basics for in depth learning.

When you finish the first level you will have seen the entire scope of Islam, The in depth knowledge will come from the next levels.

Political Islam, Not Religious Islam

Islam has a political doctrine and a religious doctrine. Its political doctrine is of concern for everyone, while religious Islam is of concern only for Muslims.

Books Designed for Learning

Each CSPI book fits into a teaching system. Most of the paragraphs have an index number which means that you can confirm for yourself how factual the books are by verifying from the original source texts.

LEVEL 1

INTRODUCTION TO THE TRILOGY AND SHARIA

The Life of Mohammed, The Hadith, Foundations of Islam, The Two Hour Koran, Sharia Law for Non-Muslims, Self Study on Political Islam, Level 1
After Level 1, you will know more about political Islam than the vast majority of people, including most experts.

LEVEL 2

APPLIED DOCTRINE, SPECIAL TOPICS

The Doctrine of Women, The Doctrine of Christians and Jews, The Doctrine of Slavery, Self-Study on Political Islam, Level 2, Psychology of the Muslim, Factual Persuasion

LEVEL 3

INTERMEDIATE TRILOGY AND SHARIA

Mohammed and the Unbelievers, Political Traditions of Mohammed, Simple Koran, Self-Study of Political Islam, Level 3, Sources of the Koran, selected topics from *Reliance of the Traveller*

LEVEL 4

ORIGINAL SOURCE TEXTS

The Life of Muhammed, Guillaume; any *Koran, Sahih Bukhari,* selected topics, *Mohammed and Charlemagne Revisited,* Scott.
With the completion of Level 4 you are prepared to read both popular and academic texts.

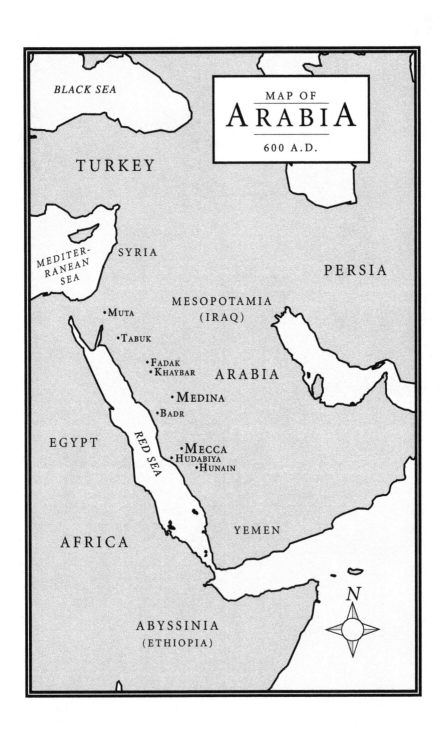

OVERVIEW

CHAPTER 1

This book will show you how Islam views Christianity and Judaism by reading the same doctrine that Islamic scholars read. This is the foundation of Islam. There is nothing deeper or more fundamental than the Koran, Sira and Hadith.

When you see Islam through the life of Mohammed, it is easy to understand. Facts are forgettable, but a story is always remembered. It all starts when Mohammed got what he called revelations from the only god. Soon stories from the Jewish scriptures emerge. You will understand the doctrine of the Jew and Christian as it unfolded in Mohammed's life. The story makes all of the pieces fit together and make sense.

THE ISLAMIC BIBLE—THE TRILOGY

Islam is defined by the words of Allah in the Koran, and the words and actions of Mohammed, called the *Sunna*.

The Sunna is found in two collections of texts—the Sira (Mohammed's life) and the Hadith. The Koran says 91 times that his words and actions are considered to be the divine pattern for humanity.

A hadith, or tradition, is a brief story about what Mohammed did or said. A collection of hadiths is called a Hadith. Only the most authoritative ones are used in this book.

So the Trilogy is the Koran, the Sira and the Hadith. Most people think that the Koran is the bible of Islam, but it is only about 14% of the total textual doctrine. This means that Islam is 14% Allah and 86% Mohammed. The Trilogy is the foundation and totality of Islam.

FIGURE1.1: THE RELATIVE SIZES OF THE TRILOGY TEXTS

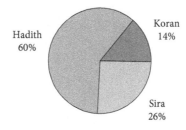

Hadith 60%
Koran 14%
Sira 26%

KAFIR

The word Kafir will be used in this book instead of "unbeliever", the standard usage. Unbeliever is a neutral term. The Koran defines the word Kafir and Kafir is not a neutral word. A Kafir is evil, disgusting, the lowest form of life. Kafirs can be deceived, hated, enslaved, tortured, killed, lied to and cheated. So the usual word "unbeliever" does not reflect the political reality of Islam.

There are many religious names for Kafirs: polytheists, idolaters, People of the Book (Christians and Jews), Buddhists, atheists, agnostics, and pagans. Kafir covers them all, because no matter what the religious name is, they can all be treated the same. What Mohammed said and did to polytheists can be done to any other category of Kafir.

Islam devotes a great amount of energy to the Kafir. The majority (64%) of the Koran is devoted to the Kafir, and nearly all of the Sira (81%) deals with Mohammed's struggle with them. The Hadith (Traditions) devotes 37% of the text to Kafirs[1]. Overall, the Trilogy devotes 51% of its content to the Kafir.

FIGURE 1.2: AMOUNT OF TEXT DEVOTED TO KAFIR

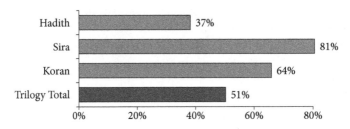

Here are a few of the Koran references:

A Kafir can be beheaded—
> Koran 47:4 *When you encounter the Kafirs on the battlefield, cut off their heads until you have thoroughly defeated them and then take the prisoners and tie them up firmly.*

A Kafir can be plotted against—
> Koran 86:15 *They plot and scheme against you [Mohammed], and I plot and scheme against them. Therefore, deal calmly with the Kafirs and leave them alone for a while.*

---

1   http://cspipublishing.com/statistical/TrilogyStats/AmtTxtDevotedKafir.html

A Kafir can be terrorized—

Koran 8:12 *Then your Lord spoke to His angels and said, "I will be with you. Give strength to the believers. I will send terror into the Kafirs' hearts, cut off their heads and even the tips of their fingers!"*

A Muslim is not the friend of a Kafir—

Koran 3:28 *Believers should not take Kafirs as friends in preference to other believers. Those who do this will have none of Allah's protection and will only have themselves as guards. Allah warns you to fear Him for all will return to Him.*

A Kafir is cursed—

Koran 33:61 *They [Kafirs] will be cursed, and wherever they are found, they will be seized and murdered. It was Allah's same practice with those who came before them, and you will find no change in Allah's ways.*

KAFIRS AND PEOPLE OF THE BOOK

Muslims tell Christians and Jews that they are not Kafirs. They are "People of the Book" and brothers in the Abrahamic faith. But in Islam, you are a Christian, if and only if, you believe that Christ was a man who was a prophet of Allah; there is no Trinity; Jesus was not crucified nor resurrected and that He will return to establish Sharia law. To be a true Jew you must believe that the Torah is corrupt, and Mohammed is the last in the line of Jewish prophets.

This verse about Christians and Jews is positive:

Koran 2:62 *Those who believe and those who are Christians and Jews and Sabians, whoever believes in Allah and Judgment Day shall have their reward with the Lord.*

Islamic doctrine is dualistic, so there is an opposite view as well. Here is the last verse written about the People of the Book (A later verse abrogates or replaces an earlier verse. See "Abrogation" on page 15.). This is the final word. It calls for Muslims to make war on the People of the Book who do not believe in the religion of truth, Islam.

Koran 9:29 *Make war on those who have received the Scriptures [Jews and Christians] but do not believe in Allah or in the Last Day. They do not forbid what Allah and His Messenger have forbidden. The Christians and Jews do not follow the religion of truth until they submit and pay the poll tax [jizya] and they are humiliated.*

The sentence "They do not forbid..." means that they do not accept Sharia law; "until they submit" means to submit to Islam and Sharia law.

Christians and Jews who do not accept Mohammed as the final prophet are Kafirs.

In Islam, Christians and Jews are infidels and "People of the Book"; Hindus are polytheists and pagans. The terms infidel, People of the Book, pagan and polytheist are religious words. Only the word "Kafir" shows the common political treatment of the Christian, Jew, Hindu, Buddhist, animist, atheist and humanist. It is simple. If you don't believe that Mohammed is the prophet of Allah, then you are a Kafir.

So, the word Kafir will be used in this book instead of "unbeliever", "non-Muslim" or "disbeliever". Unbeliever or non-Muslim are neutral terms, but Kafir is not a neutral word. It is extremely bigoted and biased.

CHRISTIANS AND JEWS

This book is intended for both Christians and Jews, but a quick scan shows that the great majority of it is about Jews. There are few mentions about Christianity. The reason is historical. Mohammed lived in Mecca until he was 53 years old. Mecca had a few Christians and almost no Jews.

In Mecca Mohammed "proved" his divine connection to a god called Allah by claiming that the angel who brought him his "revelations" was Gabriel, a Jewish angel. Therefore, Mohammed was in the linage of the Jewish prophets. There were no rabbis in Mecca to contradict him.

Then Mohammed moved to Medina, which was half Jewish. There the rabbis told him that he was no prophet in the linage of the Jews. In short, they denied his primary claim that he was a prophet of Allah.

The Jews became the enemy of Mohammed, and he annihilated them. He attacked them wherever he could. His dying words were about the Jews and Christians.

Since there were very few Christians in Arabia, they were not of political importance. Mohammed did not start attacking them until he had conquered the Arabs and crushed the Jews. If he had lived longer there would have been much more material about Christians.

The Koran mirrors this history. At first the stories of Moses, Noah, Adam and the other characters in the Jewish scriptures are retold for the purpose of showing that Allah punishes those who deny his prophets.

In the Jewish scriptures the purpose of Moses was to free the Jews, not to prove he was a prophet. In every case the story in the Jewish scriptures is reworked to show that all peoples are destroyed who deny the prophets of Allah. Indeed, the Koran written in Mecca has one theme: "Mohammed is the prophet of Allah".

4

The Koran in Medina turns on the Jews and they become the vilest of creatures. The god of the Torah loves the Jews. The god of the Medinan Koran hates the Jews. So much for the claim that the god of the Jews and the Muslims are the same god.

THE THREE VIEWS OF ISLAM

There are three points of view in dealing with Islam. The point of view depends upon how you feel about Mohammed. If you believe Mohammed is the prophet of Allah, then you are a believer. If you don't, you are a *Kafir*. The third viewpoint is that of a Kafir who is an apologist for Islam.

Apologists do not believe that Mohammed was a prophet, but they never say anything that would displease a Muslim. Apologists never offend Islam and condemn any analysis that is critical of Islam as being biased.

Let us give an example of the three points of view.

In Medina, Mohammed sat all day long beside his 12-year-old wife while they watched as the heads of 800 Jews were removed by the sword.[2] Their heads were cut off because they had said that Mohammed was not the prophet of Allah. Muslims view these deaths as necessary because denying Mohammed's prophet-hood was an offense against Islam and beheading is the accepted method of punishment, sanctioned by Allah.

Kafirs look at this event as proof of the jihadic violence of Islam and as an evil act. They call it ethnic cleansing.

Apologists say that this was a historic event, that all cultures have violence in their past, and that no judgment should be passed. They ignore the Islamic belief that the Sunna, Mohammed's words and deeds in the past, is the perfect model for today and tomorrow and forever. They ignore the fact that this past event of the beheading of 800 Jewish men continues to be acceptable in the present and the future. This example is one of the reasons that we have beheadings in the news today.

According to the different points of view, killing the 800 Jews was either evil, a perfect godly act or only another historical event, take your pick.

This book is written from the Kafir point of view and is therefore, Kafir-centric. Everything in this book views Islam from how it affects Kafirs, non-Muslims. This also means that the religion is of little importance. Only a Muslim cares about the religion of Islam, but all Kafirs are affected by Islam's political views.

---

2   *The Life of Muhammad*, A. Guillaume, Oxford University Press, 1982, pg. 464.

Notice that there is no right and wrong here, merely different points of view that cannot be reconciled. There is no possible resolution between the view of the Kafir and the Muslim. The apologist tries to bring about a bridge building compromise, but it is not logically possible.

THE REFERENCE SYSTEM

This book is unusual in that it does two things at once. It is the simplest book you can read to learn about the basic ideology. At the same time it is an authoritative because of the use of reference numbers. [Don't worry about these numbers. If you ignore them it doesn't make any difference. They are there in case you want to confirm what you have read or want to know more. The number allows you look it up in the source text. It is similar to a chapter/verse.] Here is an example:

I125 Mohammed made a decision that would have pleased Solomon. He...

The I in "I 125" tells you that it comes from Ishaq, the most authoritative writer of the Sira. The 125 is a reference number printed in the margin of the Sira. (*The Life of Muhammad*, A. Guillaume)

Other references within this work:

M123 is a page reference to W. Muir, *The Life of Mohammed*, AMS Press, 1975.

2:123 is a reference to the Koran, chapter 2, verse 123.

Bukhari1,3,4 is a reference to *Sahih Bukhari*, volume 1, book 3, number 4.

Muslim012, 1234 is a reference to *Sahih Muslim*, book 12, number 1234.

BEGINNINGS

CHAPTER 2

*4:13 These are the limits set up by Allah. Those who obey Allah
and His Messenger will be led into the Gardens watered by
flowing rivers to live forever. This is the ultimate reward!*

At age 40 Mohammed said he had his first vision of the angel
Gabriel. Mohammed told his revelations to his family and friends.
Some joined with him in Islam (submission).

There would be a Day of Judgment and those who did not worship
according to Mohammed's revelations would live in Hell.

Mohammed's attacks on the religions of Mecca caused animosity. His
opponents were promised torture for eternity. More arguments with
Meccans followed. But many` Arabs were attracted to Islam as well.

CHILDHOOD

I115[1] When Mohammed was eight years old, his grandfather died. He
was then taken in by Abu Talib, his uncle. His uncle took him on a trading trip to Syria, which was a very different place from Mecca. Syria was
a sophisticated country that was Christian and very much a part of the
cosmopolitan culture of the Mediterranean. It was Syrian Christians who
gave the Arabs their alphabet. When Mohammed was a child there were
no books written in Arabic.

MARRIAGE

I120 Mohammed was grown when he was hired by the wealthy widow
and a distant cousin Khadija to act as her agent in trading with Syria.
Mohammed had a reputation of good character and good business sense.
Trading from Mecca to Syria was risky business because it took skill to
manage a caravan and then to make the best deal in Syria. He managed
Khadija's affairs well, and she returned a good profit on the trading.

---

1.   The number is the reference to Ishaq's *Sira Rasul Allah*, the Sira, margin
note 115.

I120 Sometime after hiring Mohammed as her business agent, Khadija proposed marriage to him. They married and had six children. Their two sons died in childhood, and the four daughters lived to adulthood.

MONOTHEISM IN ARABIA

I144 After the destruction of Jerusalem by the Romans the Jews dispersed throughout the Middle East, so there was a strong presence of Jews in Arabia. There were a few Christians who were local Arabs, in fact, Mohammed's wife had a cousin who was a Christian. But the type of Christianity in the area of Mecca was unorthodox with a Trinity of God, Jesus and Mary.

I144 Jews and Christians were called the People of the Book. Since there was no book yet published in Arabic, this distinction was a strong one. The sources of the Arabic religions were found in oral tradition and custom. The Meccans were aware of the Jewish Abrahamic myths.

THE PROPHET

I150 Mohammed would take month long retreats to be alone and do the Quraysh religious practices. After the retreat he would go and circumambulate (circle and pray) at the Kabah. The Kabah was a square stone structure that had been a center for pilgrimage for centuries.

I152 At the age of forty Mohammed began to have visions and hear voices. His visions were first shown to him as bright as daybreak during his sleep in the month of Ramadan. Mohammed said that the angel, Gabriel, came to him with a brocade with writing on it and commanded him to read. The angel said:

> 96:1 Recite: In the name of your Lord, Who created man from clots of blood.
> 96:3 Recite: Your Lord is the most generous, Who taught the use of the pen and taught man what he did not know.

T1150 Mohammed awoke from his sleep. Now Mohammed hated ecstatic poets and the insane. His thoughts were that he was now either a poet or insane, that which he hated. He thought to kill himself by jumping off a cliff. And off he went to do just that. Half way up the hill, he heard, "Mohammed, You are the apostle of Allah and I am Gabriel." He gazed at the angel and no matter which way he turned his head the vision followed his eyes. Mohammed stood there for a long time.

1156 Mohammed's wife, Khadija, was the first convert. From the first she had encouraged him, believed him. She knew him to be of good character and did not think him to be deceived or crazy.

PRAYER

1157 Mohammed began to do his prayers with his new understanding. At first he did two prostrations with each prayer. Later he understood that he should use four prostrations per prayer and use two prostrations when he was traveling.

1158 Then when he was on a mountain he saw a vision in which Gabriel showed him how to do ritual ablutions as a purification ritual before prayer. He went home and showed his wife, Khadija, how he now understood the prayer rituals to be done and she copied him.

The following seven verses are used as a prayer, five times a day:

> 1:1 *In the Name of Allah, the Compassionate, the Merciful.*
> 1:2 *Praise be to Allah, Lord of the worlds. The Compassionate, the Merciful. King of the Judgment Day.*
> 1:5 *Only You do we worship, and to You alone do we ask for help. Keep us on the straight and narrow path. The path of those that You favor; not the path of those who anger You [the Jews] nor the path of those who go astray [the Christians].*

PREACHING

One of the many gods in Mecca was Allah, a moon god. The native religions did not have any formal structure for the many deities, but Allah was a high god. Allah was the primary god of the Quraysh tribe of Mohammed, and Mohammed's father was named Abdullah, slave of Allah.

Mohammed preached the doctrine of the Day of Judgment. The Koran:

> 83:10 *Woe on that day [Judgment day] to those who deny Our signs, who regard the Judgment Day as a lie! No one regards it as a lie except the transgressor or the criminal, who, when Our signs are recited to him, says, "Old wives tales!" No! Their habits have become like rust on their hearts. Yes, they will be veiled from their Lord's light that day. Then they will be burned in Hell. They will be told, "This is what you called a lie."*

After the Day of Doom would come Paradise and Hell.

> 52:7 *Truly, a punishment from your Lord is coming, and no one can stop it. That day heaven will heave from side to side, and the mountains will shake to pieces. Woe on that day to those who called the messengers liars, who wasted their time in vain disputes.*

52:13 On that day they will be thrown into the Fire of Hell. This is the Fire that you treated like a lie. What! Do you think that this is magic? Or, do you not see it? Burn there! Bear it patiently, or impatiently. It will all be the same to you, because you will certainly get what you deserve.

52:17 But those who have feared Allah will live pleasantly amid Gardens, rejoicing in what their Lord has given them, and what their Lord has protected them from, saying, "Eat and drink in health as a reward for your good deeds." They will recline on arranged couches, and We will marry them to dark-eyed houris [beautiful companions of pleasure].

I161 Any person who rejected the revelations of Mohammed would be eternally punished. The culture of religious tolerance in Mecca now had a new religion which preached the end of tolerance. Only Islam was acceptable.

I166 Mohammed began to openly preach his new doctrine. He had been private for three years before he went public.

The Arabs had always believed in jinns, invisible beings created from fire. Now they appeared in the Koran.

51:56 I created jinn [creatures made from fire] and man only to worship me. I need no livelihood from them, and I do not need them to feed me. Truly, Allah is the sole sustainer, the possessor of power, and the unmovable!

I166 The Muslims went to the edge of Mecca to pray in order to be alone. One day a group of the Quraysh came upon them and began to mock then and a fight started. Saed, a Muslim, picked up the jaw bone of a camel, struck one of the Quraysh with it, and bloodied him. This violence was the first blood to be shed in Islam.

I167 When Mohammed spoke about his new religion, it did not cause any problems among the Meccans. Then Mohammed began to condemn their religion, rituals, and worship. The Meccans took offense and resolved to treat him as an enemy. Luckily, he had the protection of his influential uncle, Abu Talib.

I170 Things got much worse. Now there was open hostility in the town. Quarrels increased, arguments got very heated. Complete disharmony dominated the town. The tribe started to abuse the recently converted Muslims. But Mohammed's uncle Abu Talib was a respected elder and was able to protect them from real harm.

This is the Sunna of Mohammed

PUBLIC TEACHING

3:32 Say: Obey Allah and His messenger, but if they reject it,
then truly, Allah does not love those who reject the faith.

SUMMARY

As Mohammed continued to preach Islam, more arguments happened. The only true religion was Islam. Mohammed's opponents were doomed to Hell.

The leaders tried to prove Mohammed wrong with arguments and demands for heavenly proof. Mohammed continued to argue that the Koran was the only proof of his divine mission that was needed.

The Koran continued in its insistence that Mohammed was the prophet of Allah. All the resistance to the words of Mohammed was evil.

The Meccans arguments continued. They asked why the Koran was not delivered in a complete form? The Koran condemns those who argue with Mohammed:

> 25:32 *Those who disbelieve say, "Why wasn't the Koran revealed to him all at once?" It was revealed one part at a time so that We might strengthen your heart with it and so that We might rehearse it with you gradually, in slow, well-arranged stages.*
>
> 25:33 *They will not come to you with any difficult questions for which We have not provided you the true and best answers. Those who will be gathered together face down in Hell will have the worst place and will be the farthest away from the right path.*

The Meccans had many leaders who resisted Mohammed.

> 38:55 *But the evil have a terrible place waiting for them—Hell—where they will be burned. What a wretched bed to lie on! Let them taste boiling water and icy fluid and other vile things. Their leaders will be told, "This group will be thrown head first into the fire with you. There is no welcome for them. They will burn in the fire!"*

I183 One day at the Kabah the Meccans were discussing Mohammed and his enmity towards them, when Mohammed arrived. The Meccans insulted him. He said, "Listen to me, by Allah I will bring you slaughter." The Quraysh were stunned at his threat. They said, "Mohammed, you have never been a violent man, go away."

I184 The next day many of the Quraysh were at the Kabah when Mohammed arrived. They crowded around him and said, "Are you the one who condemned our gods and our religion?" Mohammed answered that he was the one. One of them grabbed him and Abu Bakr, Mohammed's chief follower, pressed forward and said, "Would you kill a man for saying that Allah is his Lord?" They let him go. Mecca was a small town and there were meetings about what to do about Mohammed.

> 43:79 *Do they make plots against you? We also make plots. Do they think that We do not hear their secrets and their private conversations? We do, and Our messengers are there to record them.*

He continued to speak of Allah and the Koran. Many times in the Koran, we find self-proofs of the validity of the Koran and the proof of Allah.

> 67:2 *You can not see one defect in merciful Allah's creation. Do you see a crack in the sky? Look again and again. Your vision will blur from looking, but you will find no defects.*

MORE ARGUMENTS WITH THE MECCANS

I188,189 Another group of Meccans sent for Mohammed to see if they could negotiate away this painful division of the tribes. They went over old ground and again Mohammed refused the money and power that was offered. He said they were the ones who needed to decide whether they wanted to suffer in the next world and he had the only solution. If they rejected him and his message, Allah would tend to them. One of the Quraysh said, "Well, this land is dry. Let his Allah send them a river next to Mecca. Have Allah move the mountains back from Mecca. Have Allah bring Qusayy, our best leader, back to life."

I189 Mohammed said that he was sent as a messenger, not to do such work. They could either accept his message or reject it and be subject to the loss. Then one of them said, "Send an angel to confirm you and prove to us that we are wrong. As long as the angel was present, let him make Mohammed a garden and fine home and present him with all the gold and silver he needed. If you do this, we will know that you represent Allah and we are wrong." The Quraysh wanted miracles as a proof.

15:4 *We never destroy a city whose term wasn't preordained. No nation can delay or change its destiny. They say: "You [Mohammed] to whom the message was revealed, you are surely insane. If you were telling the truth, why didn't you bring angels to us?"*

15:8 *We do not send the angels without good reason. If We did, the Kafirs would still not understand. Surely, We have sent down the message, and surely, We will guard it. Before your time, We sent apostles to the sects of the ancient peoples, but they mocked every messenger. Similarly, We allow doubt to enter the hearts of the sinners.*

I189 Mohammed did not do miracles, because such things were not what Allah had appointed him to do.

I189 Then one of the Quraysh said, "Then let the heavens be dropped on us in pieces as you say your Lord could do. Then if you do not we will not believe." Mohammed said that Allah could do that if Allah wished or he might not if he wished.

I189 They then said, "Did not your Lord know that we would ask you these questions? Then your Lord could have prepared you with better answers. And your Lord could have told you what to tell us if we don't believe. We hear that you are getting this Koran from a man named Al Rahman from another town. We don't believe in Al Rahman. Our conscience is clear. We must either destroy you or you must destroy us. Bring your angels and we will believe them."

I191 Mohammed would come to the Kabah and tell the Meccans what terrible punishments that Allah had delivered to the others in history who had not believed their prophets. That was now one of his constant themes. Allah destroyed others like the Meccans who did not listen to men like Mohammed.

A punishment story:

23:40 *Allah said, "In a short time they will quickly repent." Then the justice of the awful blast overtook them, and We turned them into so much rubbish swept away by a flood. So away with the wicked.*

23:42 *After them, We created other generations. No people may either hasten or delay their appointed time. Then We sent Our messengers one after another. Every time a messenger went forth to a nation, its people accused him of lying, so We caused them to follow one another into disaster, and We made them examples. So, away with the Kafirs.*

Moses:

79:20 *And Moses showed Pharaoh a great miracle. But Pharaoh denied it and disobeyed. Furthermore, he turned his back and rebelled against Allah. He gathered an army and made a proclamation, saying, "I am your lord, the most high." So Allah punished him and made an example of him in this life and the hereafter. Surely this is a lesson for those who fear Allah.*

A story about Abraham with Ishmael as the sacrifice:

37:102 *When the son [Ishmael] grew tall enough to work, his father said to him, "Son, a dream tells me that I should sacrifice you. What do you think?" He said, "Father, do what you are commanded. If Allah wills, you will find me patient."*

I192 Since Mohammed and the Koran claimed Jewish roots, the Quraysh decided to send their story teller to the Jews in Medina and ask for help.

I192 The rabbis said, "Ask him these three questions. If he knows the answer then he is a prophet, if not then he is a fake."

"What happened to the young men who disappeared in ancient days."

"Ask him about the mighty traveler who reached the ends of the East and the West."

"Ask him, What is the spirit?"

I192 Back in Mecca, they went to Mohammed and asked him the three questions. He said he would get back to them tomorrow. Days went by. Finally, fifteen days had passed. Mohammed waited on Gabriel for the answers. The Meccans began to talk. Mohammed did not know what to do. He had no answers. Finally, he had a vision of Gabriel.

19:64 *The angels say, "We descend from heaven only by Allah's command. Everything that is before us and everything that is behind us and whatever is in between belongs to Him. And Your Lord never forgets."*

The Koran answered all the questions and statements of the Quraysh. With regards to the question about what happened to the young men in ancient times [this was a well know ancient tale], it says:

18:25 *They remained in their cave for three hundred years, though some say three hundred and nine. Say: Allah knows exactly how long they stayed. He knows the secrets of the heavens and the earth. Man has no guardian besides Him. He does not allow any to share His power.*

As to the question about the mighty traveler, Alexander the Great:

18:83 *They will ask you about Zul-Qarnain [Alexander the Great]. Say: I will recite to you an account of him. We established his power in the land and gave him the means to achieve any of his aims. So he followed a path, until, when he reached the setting of the sun, he found it setting in a muddy pond. Near by he found a people. We said, "Zul-Qarnain, you have the authority to either punish them or to show them kindness."*

According to the Koran Alexander the Great was a prophet of Allah.

The question—what is the spirit?

> 17:85 *They will ask you about the spirit [probably the angel Gabriel]. Say: The spirit is commanded by my Lord, and you are given only a little knowledge about it.*

After the Jewish leaders in Medina helped the Meccans with questions to ask Mohammed, the Koran has its first negative comments about the Jews.

> 5:64 *The Jews say, "The hand of Allah is chained up." Their own hands will be chained up [on the Last Day, the Jews would have their right hand chained to their necks], and they will be cursed for what they say.*

ABROGATION

The change in the Koran about Jews was noticed. About this time the Meccans started pointing out to Mohammed that his Koran said one thing before and says something different later.

> 16:101 *When We exchange one verse for another, and Allah knows best what He reveals, they say, "You are making this up." Most of them do not understand.*

> 2:106 *Whatever of Our revelations We repeal or cause to be forgotten, We will replace with something superior or comparable. [There are as many as 225 verses of the Koran that are altered by later verses. This is called abrogation.]*

In general, abrogation means that a later verse nullifies or weakens an earlier contradictory verse. However, since both come from Allah they can both be used when needed. In truth, this leads to dualism—two contradictory ideas which are both true.

This is the Sunna of Mohammed

STRUGGLES

CHAPTER 4

*8:20 Believers! Be obedient to Allah and His messenger, and
do not turn your backs now that you know the truth. Do
not be like the ones who say, "We hear," but do not obey.*

SUMMARY

The Meccans began to resist Mohammed. Again and again the
Koran condemned all those who resisted Islam to eternal torture
in Hell.

More Meccans began to believe Mohammed. There was a larger
gulf between Muslims and their old friends.

Mohammed had his most famous visions, the night journey to
Paradise.

Mohammed's uncle and wife died. Mohammed soon had a new
bride.

I235 A Meccan met Mohammed and said, "Mohammed, you stop cursing our gods or we will start cursing your Allah." So Mohammed stopped
cursing the Meccan gods. An ongoing theme of Mohammed's was of ancient civilizations who did not listen to their prophets and the terrible
downfall of that country.

> *11:59 The men of Ad [an ancient people of southern Arabia] rejected signs
> of their Lord, rebelled against His messengers, and followed the bidding of
> every proud, defiant person. They were cursed in this world, and on Res-
> urrection Day it will be said to them, "Did Ad not reject their Lord?" The
> people of Ad were cast far away.*

THE SATANIC VERSES

I239 Some Meccans approached Mohammed and said, "Let us worship
what you worship. Then you worship what we worship. If what you worship is better than what we worship, then we will take a share of your
worship. And if what we worship is better, then you can take a share of
that."

T1192[1] Mohammed was always thinking of how he could persuade all the Meccans. It came to him that the three gods of the Quraysh could intercede with Allah. The Meccans were delighted and happy. When Mohammed lead prayers at the Kabah, all the Meccans, Muslim and Kafir, took part. The Quraysh hung about after the combined service and remarked how happy they were.

T1192 But it was Satan had made him say those terrible words about how the other gods could help Allah. The retraction by Mohammed made the relations between Islam and the Meccans far worse than it had ever been.

> 22:52 Never have We sent a prophet or messenger before you whom Satan did not tempt with evil desires, but Allah will bring Satan's temptations to nothing. Allah will affirm His revelations, for He is knowing and wise. He makes Satan's suggestions a temptation for those whose hearts are diseased or for those whose hearts are hardened.

HELL

The Koran's most descriptive language is reserved for Hell. Hell occupies a large part of the Koran, particularly the early Meccan Koran. There are 217 verses that directly refer to Hell.

> 22:19 These two, the believers and the Kafirs, argue with each other about their Lord, but for the Kafirs, clothing of Fire has been made for them. Boiling water will be poured on their heads. It will scald their insides and their skin as well. They will be beaten with iron rods. Every time they, in their torment, attempt to escape from the Fire, they will be dragged back into it, and they will be told, "Taste the torture of the burning."

PREDESTINATION

Again and again the Koran proclaims the total control of Allah over the smallest action.

> 7:178,179 Those whom Allah guides are on the right path; those whom He leaves in error are the losers. We have created many jinn and men to burn in Hell.

However, some few verses imply free will. Dualism is one of the principles of the Koran.

> 18:29 Say: the truth is from your Lord; whoever wills may believe, and whoever wills may disbelieve.

---

1. The T references are to Al Tabari's *History of Prophets and Kings*

THE POET'S SUBMISSION

I252 Al Dausi was a poet of some standing in Arabia and he decided to submit to Islam. He returned home. His father was old and came to greet his son. Al Dausi said to him, "Go away father, for I want nothing to do with you or you with me." His father said, "Why, my son?" Al Dausi said, "I have become a Muslim." The father replied, "Well, then I shall do so as well."

I253 He then entered his home and told his wife, "Leave me, I want nothing to do with you." She cried, "Why?" Al Dausi said, "Islam has divided us and I now follow Mohammed." She replied, "Then your religion is my religion." He then instructed her in Islam.

The Koran is constant in its admonitions that Muslims should not be friends with Kafirs. [There are 12 verses that say this.]

> 3:28 *Believers should not take Kafirs as friends in preference to other believers. Those who do this will have none of Allah's protection and will only have themselves as guards. Allah warns you to fear Him for all will return to Him.*

> 5:57 *Oh, you who believe, do not take those who have received the Scriptures [Jews and Christians] before you, who have scoffed and jested at your religion, or who are Kafirs for your friends. Fear Allah if you are true believers. When you call to prayer, they make it a mockery and a joke. This is because they are a people who do not understand.*

I260 In the market there was a Christian slave who ran a booth. Mohammed would go and speak with him at length. This led to the Quraysh saying that what Mohammed said in the Koran, came from the Christian slave. The Koran's response:

> 16:102 *Say: The Holy Spirit [Gabriel] has truthfully revealed it from your Lord so that it may confirm the faith of those who believe and be a guide and good news for those who submit. We know that they say, "It is a man that teaches him." The man [his name is uncertain] they point to speaks a foreign language while this is clear Arabic.*

THE NIGHT JOURNEY

> 17:1 *Glory to Allah, Who took His servant on a night time journey from the Sacred Mosque in Mecca to the furthest Mosque [Jerusalem], whose neighborhood We have blessed so that We might show him Our signs: He, and only He, hears and sees all things.*

I264 One night as Mohammed lay sleeping, Gabriel woke him and took his arm. They went out the door and found a white animal, half mule and half donkey. Its feet had wings and could move to the horizon at one step. Gabriel put Mohammed on the white animal and off they went to Jerusalem to the site of the Temple.

1264 There at the temple were Jesus, Abraham, Moses, and other prophets. Mohammed led them in prayer.

1265 When Mohammed told this story at the Kabah, the Quraysh hooted at the absurdity of it. Aisha, Mohammed's favorite wife, used to say that Mohammed never left the bed that night, however, his spirit soared.

1266 Mohammed reported that Abraham looked exactly like him. Moses was a ruddy faced man, tall, thin, and with curly hair. Jesus was light skinned with reddish complexion and freckles and lank hair.

1269 At the lowest heaven, a Adam sat with the spirits of men passing in front of him. He was reviewing the spirits of his children. The spirit of a Muslim excited him and the spirit of a Kafir disgusted him.

1270 Then Mohammed was taken up to the second heaven and saw Jesus and his cousin, John, son of Zakariah. In the third heaven he saw Joseph, son of Jacob. In the fourth heaven, Mohammed saw Idris. In the fifth heaven was a man was Aaron, son of Imran. In the sixth heaven was Moses. In the seventh heaven was a man sitting on a throne in front of a mansion. Every day 70,000 angels went into the mansion, not to come out until the day of resurrection. The man on the throne looked just like Mohammed; it was Abraham.

1271 When Gabriel took Mohammed to each of the heavens and asked permission to enter he had to say who he had brought and whether they had a mission. They would then say, "Allah grant him life, brother and friend." When Mohammed got to the seventh heaven his Lord gave him the duty of fifty prayers a day. Moses persuaded him to ask for a reduction. Allah reduced the number to five. In the Night Journey, Mohammed is portrayed as the successor to the Jewish prophets.

Mohammed is the final prophet, and the Koran is pure and perfect, whereas the Jewish and Christian scripture have been corrupted. Jews and Christians must submit to Islam. The Koran continues and perfects the Scriptures.

1272 One day Mohammed stood with the angel, Gabriel, as the Quraysh performed the rituals of their religion. Among them were the leaders who defended their native culture and religion and opposed Mohammed. When the first leader passed by Gabriel, Gabriel threw a leaf in his face and blinded him. Gabriel then caused the second one to get dropsy which killed him. The third man Gabriel caused him to develop an infection which killed him. The fourth man was caused later to step on a thorn which killed him. Gabriel used a brain disease to kill the last leader who denied Mohammed

FAMILY

Abu Talib, Mohammed's uncle, had taken the orphan into his home and raised him. He took Mohammed on caravan trading missions to Syria and taught him how to be a businessman. Abu Talib was the clan chief who protected Mohammed's life when the rest of Mecca wanted to harm him. He was Mohammed's life and security, but when he died, Mohammed damned him to Hell.

After Abu Talib's death, the pressure on Mohammed intensified. It reached the point where one of the Quraysh threw dust at Mohammed.

The death of his wife, Khadija, had no political effect, but it was a blow to Mohammed. His wife was his chief confidant, and she consoled him.

MARRIAGE

About three months after the death of Khadija Mohammed married Sauda, a widow and a Muslim.

Abu Bakr had a six year old daughter, Aisha. She was to become his favorite wife. The consummation would not take place until she turned nine.

> Muslim031,5977 *Aisha reported Mohammed having said: I saw you in a dream for three nights when an angel brought you to me in a silk cloth and he said: Here is your wife, and when I removed (the cloth) from your face, lo, it was yourself, so I said: If this is from Allah, let Him carry it out.*

This is the Sunna of Mohammed

POLITICAL BEGINNINGS

CHAPTER 5

24:52 It is such as obey Allah and His Apostle, and fear
Allah and do right, that will win (in the end).

SUMMARY

Mohammed began to seek political allies. He made a political alliance with the new Muslims from Medina, a nearby town. Formal pledges were made that recognized Mohammed as a political leader.

Plans were made to leave Mecca and immigrate to Medina.

In Medina Mohammed set up a political charter which established a dualistic legal and ethical system. He then consummated his marriage to Aisha when she was nine years old.

Some of the Medinans submitted to Islam and then had doubts. Those who doubted were called hypocrites.

I279 With Abu Talib's death, Mohammed needed political allies. Mohammed went to the city of Taif, about fifty miles away, with one servant. In Taif he met with three brothers who were politically powerful.

I279 One brother said that if Mohammed were the representative of Allah, then the brother would go and rip off the covering of the Kabah, Allah's shrine. The second brother said, "Couldn't Allah have found someone better than Mohammed to be a prophet?" The third brother said, "Don't let me even speak to you. If you are the prophet of Allah as you say you are, then you are too important for me to speak with. And if you are not, then you are lying. And it is not right to speak with liars."

I280 Since they could not agree, Mohammed asked them to keep their meeting private. Mohammed kept condemning them and their kind, until one day a mob gathered and drove him out of town, pelting him with stones.

THE BEGINNING OF POWER AND JIHAD IN MEDINA

Medina was about a ten-day journey from Mecca, but since ancient times the Medinans had come to Mecca for the fairs. Medina was half Jewish and half Arabian, and there was an ongoing tension between the two. The Jews worked as farmers and craftsmen and were literate. They were the wealthy class, but their power was slowly waning. The Jews said that one day a prophet would come and lead them to victory over the Arabs. In spite of the tensions, the Arab tribe of Khazraj were allies with the Jews.

1286 So when the members of the Khazraj met Mohammed, they said among themselves, "This is the prophet the Jews spoke of. Let us join ranks with him before the Jews do." They hoped that Islam could unite them, and soon every house in Medina had heard of Islam.

1289 The next year when the Medinan Muslims returned to Mecca, they took an oath to Mohammed. They returned to Medina, and soon many of Medinans submitted to Islam.

1294 At the next fair in Mecca, many of the new Muslims from Medina showed up. During the early part of the night about seventy of them left the caravan to meet with Mohammed. He recited the Koran and said, "I invite your allegiance on the basis that you protect me as you would your children." The Medinans gave their oath. After the oath, one of them asked about their now severed ties to the Jews of Medina. If they helped Mohammed with arms and they were successful would he go back to Mecca? Mohammed smiled and said, "No, blood is blood, and blood not to be paid for is blood not to be paid for." Blood revenge and its obligation were common to them. "I will war against them that war against you and be at peace with those at peace with you."

1299 One of the Medinans said to those who made the pledge, "Do you realize what your are committing your selves to with this man? It is war against all." They asked what they would receive for their oath, Mohammed promised them Paradise. They all shook hands on the deal.

MIGRATION

1304 Back in Medina the Muslims now practiced their new religion openly. But most of the Arabs still practiced their ancient tribal religions. The Muslims would desecrate the old shrines and ritual objects. They would even break into houses and steal the ritual objects and throw them into the latrines. On one occasion they killed a dog and tied the dog's body to the ritual object and thew it into the latrine.

1313 Up to now the main tension in the division in the Quraysh tribe over the new religion had been resolved by words. What blood had been drawn had been in the equivalent of a brawl. Dust had been thrown, but no real violence. No one had died.

1314 The Muslim Medinans had pledged Mohammed support in war and to help the Muslims from Mecca. The Muslims in Mecca left and went to Medina. The Muslims from both Mecca and Medina were about to be tested.

I324-326 The Quraysh feared that Mohammed and his Medinan allies would war with the Quraysh and Mecca. So the Quraysh assembled as a council in order to figure out what to do. In the end the Quraysh let the Muslims go. The Quraysh wanted the their problem to go away.

> 8:30 *Remember the Kafirs who plotted against you and sought to have you taken prisoner or to have you killed or banished. They made plans, as did Allah, but Allah is the best plotter of all.*

I336-337 In Medina Mohammed set to work building the first mosque. There were now two groups of Muslims in Medina, the Quraysh Migrants from Mecca and the Helpers from Medina.

THE COVENANT

I341 Mohammed wrote up a charter or covenant for a basis of law and government. The religion of Islam now had a political system. Islam now had power over those outside the mosque. All Muslims, whether from Mecca, Medina or anywhere else, were part of a community, umma, that excluded others. There was one set of ethics for the Muslims and another set for the Kafirs. Duality was established as a fundamental principle of Islamic ethics.

I341 Muslims should oppose any who would sow discord among other Muslims. A Muslim should not kill another Muslim, nor should he help a Kafir against a Muslim. Muslims are friends to each other, to the exclusion of Kafirs. Muslims shall avenge blood shed of another Muslim in jihad. A non-believer shall not intervene against a Muslim.

I342 The Jews who align themselves with Mohammed are to be treated fairly. Jews are to help pay for war if they are fighting with the Muslims as allies. No Jew may go to war without the permission of Mohammed, except for revenge killings. Jews must help Muslims if they are attacked. All trouble and controversy must be judged by Mohammed. No Meccans are to be aided.

MARRIAGE

About seven months after arriving in Medina Mohammed, aged fifty-three, consummated his marriage with Aisha, now age nine. She was allowed to bring her dolls into the harem due to her age.

THE HYPOCRITES

1351 Before Mohammed arrived, the Arabs who practiced their ancient religions were content with their religion and tolerant of others. Many Arabs became Muslims due to a pressure to join Islam. But in secret they were hypocrites who allied themselves with the Jews because they thought Mohammed was deluded.

1365 The Koran gives an analogy about the hypocrites:

> 2:8 And some of the people [the Jews] say, "We believe in Allah and the Day," although they do not really believe. They wish to deceive Allah and His believers, but they fool no one but themselves although they do not know it. Their hearts are diseased, and Allah has increased their suffering. They will suffer an excruciating doom because of their lies.

1358 One of the hypocrites excused his criticism by saying that he was only talking and jesting. No criticism was too small to be unnoticed.

> 9:65 If you ask them, they will surely say, "We were only talking idly and jesting." Say: Do you mock Allah, His signs, and His Messenger? Make no excuse. You have rejected faith after you accepted it. If we forgive some of you, we will punish others because they are evildoers.

1365 The hypocrites change their faces depending upon who they are with. When they are with the Muslims, they believe. But when they are with the evil ones (the Jews) they say they are with the Jews. It is the Jews who order them to deny the truth and contradict Mohammed.

This is the Sunna of Mohammed

THE JEWS

CHAPTER 6

*9:63 Do they not know that whoever opposes Allah
and His Messenger will abide in the Fire of Hell, where
they will remain forever? This is the great shame.*

SUMMARY

The Jews comprised about half of Medina. In Mecca Mohammed claimed the mantle of the Jewish tradition of being a prophet. But the Jews in Medina said that Mohammed was not their prophet. Then Mohammed claimed that the Jews were corrupt and that only he knew the actual doctrine of the Jewish scriptures.

Now the Koran and Mohammed began to attack the Jews and the direction of Islamic prayer was changed from Jerusalem to Mecca.

When Mohammed came to Medina about half the town was Jewish. There were three tribes of Jews and two tribes of Arabs. The Jews were farmers and tradesmen and lived in their own fortified quarters. In general they were better educated and more prosperous than the Arabs.

Before Mohammed arrived, there had been bad blood and killing among the tribes. The last battle had been fought by the two Arab tribes, but each of the Jewish tribes had joined the battle with their particular Arab allies. In addition to that tension between the two Arab tribes, there was a tension between the Jews and the Arabs.

These quarrelsome tribal relationships were one of the reasons that Mohammed was invited to Medina. But the result was further polarization, not unity. The new split was between Islam and those Arabs and their Jewish partners who resisted Islam.

I351 About this time, the leaders of the Jews spoke out against Mohammed. The rabbis began to ask him difficult questions. Doubts about Allah were evil. However, two of the Jews joined with Mohammed as Muslims. They believed him when he said that he was the Jewish prophet that came to fulfill the Torah.

THE REAL TORAH IS IN THE KORAN

Mohammed said repeatedly that the Jews and Christians corrupted their sacred texts in order to conceal the fact that he was prophesied in their scriptures. The stories in the Koran are similar to those of the Jew's scriptures, but they make different points. In the Koran, all of the stories found in Jewish scripture indicated that Allah destroyed those cultures that did not listen to their messengers. According to Mohammed, the scriptures of the Jews had been changed to hide the fact that Islam is the true religion.

1367 Mohammed is the final prophet. His coming was in the original Torah. Allah has blessed the Jews and protected them and now they refuse to believe the final and perfect prophet. The Jews are not ignorant, but deceitful. The Jews know the truth of Mohammed and cover the truth and hide the truth with lies.

> 2:40 Children of Israel! Remember the favor I have given you, and keep your covenant with Me. I will keep My covenant with you. Fear My power. Believe in what I reveal [the Koran], which confirms your Scriptures, and do not be the first to disbelieve it. Do not part with My revelations for a petty price. Fear Me alone. Do not mix up the truth with lies or knowingly hide the truth [Mohammed said the Jews hid their scriptures that foretold Mohammed would be the final prophet].

1367 The Koran repeats the many favors that Allah has done for the Jews—they were the chosen people, delivered from slavery under the pharaoh, given the sacred Torah and all they have ever done is to sin. They have been forgiven many times by Allah, and still, they are as hard as rocks and refuse to believe Mohammed. They have perverted the Torah after understanding it.

> 2:75 Can you believers then hope that the Jews will believe you even though they heard the Word of Allah and purposefully altered it [the Koran says that the true Torah prophesied the coming of Mohammed] after they understood its meaning? And when they are among the believers they say, "We believe too," but when they are alone with one another they say, "Will you tell them what Allah has revealed to you so that they can argue with you about it in the presence of your Lord?" Do you not have any sense? Do they not realize that Allah knows what they hide as well as what they reveal?

1369 The Jews' sins are so great that Allah has changed them into apes. Still they will not learn and refuse to admit that Mohammed is their prophet. They know full well the truth and hide and confuse others. Even when they say to Mohammed they believe, they conceal their resistance.

> 2:63 *And remember, Children of Israel, when We made a covenant with you and raised Mount Sinai before you saying, "Hold tightly to what We have revealed to you and keep it in mind so that you may guard against evil." But then you turned away, and if it had not been for Allah's grace and mercy, you surely would have been among the lost. And you know those among you who sinned on the Sabbath. We said to them, "You will be transformed into despised apes." So we used them as a warning to their people and to the following generations, as well as a lesson for the Allah-fearing.*

> Muslim042,7135 *Mohammed said, "A tribe of Bani Isra'il [Jews] disappeared. I do not know what became of them, but I think they mutated and became rats. Have you noticed that a rat won't drink camel's milk, but they will drink goat's milk?"*

1370 The Jews have understood the truth of Mohammed and then changed their scriptures to avoid admitting that Mohammed is right. The Koran often uses the term People of the Book. At the time of Mohammed there were no books in Arabic. The written Arabic was used mostly for business. Since both Christianity and Judaism used religious texts this was distinctive. The term People of the Book can refer to either Jews, Christians, or both Jews and Christians.

> 5:59 *Say: Oh, people of the Book [Jews and Christians], do you not reject us only because we believe in Allah, in what He has sent down to us, in what He has sent before us, and because most of you are wrongdoers? Say: Can I tell you of retribution worse than this that awaits them with Allah? It is for those who incurred the curse of Allah and His anger; those whom He changed into apes and swine; those who worship evil are in a worse place, and have gone far astray from the right path.*

> 5:82 *You will find the Jews and the polytheists to be the most passionately hostile to those who believe. You will find the Christians to be the nearest in affection to those who believe. This is because they are devoted men of learning, and they are not arrogant.*

MOHAMMED TRULY FOLLOWS THE RELIGION OF ABRAHAM

1381 Christians and Jews argued with Mohammed that if he wished to have salvation, then he would have to convert. But Mohammed is the one who truly follows the religion of Abraham. Mohammed is the true Jew with the true Torah.

> 3:66 *Abraham was neither a Jew nor a Christian, but a righteous man, a Muslim, not an idol worshipper. Doubtless the ones who follow Abraham are the closest to him, along with this messenger and the believers. Allah is protector of the faithful. Some of the People of the Book try to lead you astray, but they only mislead themselves, although they may not realize it.*

1397 Three Jews came to Mohammed and said, "Do you not allege that you follow the religion of Abraham and believe in the Torah which we have and testify that it is the truth from Allah?" He replied, "Certainly, but you have sinned and broken the covenant contained therein and concealed what you were ordered to make plain to men. I disassociate myself from your sin (concealing the part of the Torah that prophesied the coming of Ahmed (a variation of the name Mohammed)".

It is Islam that defines the Jews and Christians. Christians and Jews must submit politically and theologically to Islam.

> 4:47 *To those of you [Jews and Christians] to whom the Scriptures were given: Believe in what We have sent down confirming the Scriptures you already possess before We destroy your faces and twist your heads around backwards, or curse you as We did those [the Jews] who broke the Sabbath for Allah's commandments will be carried out.*

The Koran mentions a Jew who converted to Islam.

> 46:9 *I am not Allah's first messenger, nor do I know what He will do with me and you. I follow what is revealed to me through inspiration, and my charge is to warn you [the Meccans]. What do you think? This Scripture is from Allah, and you reject it, and a witness [a Jew, bin Salama] from the Children of Israel testifies that he has seen earlier scripture like it and believes it, while you proudly show scorn. Surely, Allah does not guide the unjust.*

AN OMINOUS CHANGE

1381 In Mecca Mohammed spoke well of the Jews, who were very few. In Medina there were many Jews and his relations were tense. Up to now Mohammed had lead prayer in the direction of Jerusalem. Now the Kibla, direction of prayer, was changed to the Kabah in Mecca.

1382 Mohammed summoned the Jews to Islam and made it attractive and warned them of Allah's punishment and vengeance. The Jews said that they would follow the religion of their fathers. Since Islam is the successor to Judaism, Allah was the successor to Jehovah. It was actually Allah who had been the deity of the Jews and the Jews had deliberately hidden this fact by corrupted scriptures. For this the Jews will be cursed.

62:5 *Those to whom the Torah [the first five books of the Old Testament] was given and do not follow it can be compared to a donkey who is made to carry a load of books but is unable to understand them. Those who reject Allah's revelations are a sorry example. Allah does not guide those who do wrong.*

4:47 *To those of you [Jews and Christians] to whom the Scriptures were given: Believe in what We have sent down confirming the Scriptures you already possess before We destroy your faces and twist your heads around backwards, or curse you as We did those [the Jews were changed into apes] who broke the Sabbath for Allah's commandments will be carried out.*

The Kafirs will burn forever in the fire of Hell.

98:6 *The Kafirs among the People of the Book and the idolaters will burn for eternity in the Fire of Hell. Of all the created beings, they are the most despicable. As for those who believe and do good works, they are the most noble of all created beings.*

This is the Sunna of Mohammed

JIHAD, WAR AGAINST ALL

CHAPTER 7

*4:42 On that day, the Kafirs and those who disobeyed
the Messenger will wish they could sink into the earth
for they cannot hide a single thing from Allah.*

SUMMARY

After a year in Medina, Mohammed sent his armed men out to attack the caravans of his old enemies, the Meccans.

On their eighth attempt, the Muslims were successful by using deceit to attack a caravan in a sacred month.

Later a new Meccan caravan was due to pass near Medina, and Mohammed decided to strike his enemies and raid it. But the caravan leader was fearful and sent a fast rider to Mecca for armed help. Mohammed's army and the Meccan fighters camped near Badr.

Mohammed gave the order and the battle started. The Muslims were outnumbered, but fought with courage. Islam was triumphant and some of Mohammed's old enemies were killed.

War was instituted as a permanent strategy of Islamic politics.

Immediately after winning at Badr, Mohammed sent out warriors on other raids.

I415 It was thirteen years after he started preaching and a year after going to Medina that Mohammed prepared for war as commanded by Allah.

THE FIRST RAIDS

I416-423 Mohammed sent forth his fighters on seven armed raids to find the trade caravans headed to Mecca.

JIHAD—THE FIRST KILLING

I423-4 Mohammed sent Abdullah out with eight men. A caravan of the Quraysh passed by the Muslims as they overlooked the road from a rise. When the Quraysh saw them they were scared, but one of the Muslims had a shaved head. Now a shaved head was a mark of pilgrim so the Quraysh felt better. They were safe. They were also in a sacred month when weapons were not carried.

1425 The Muslims took council. They were in a dilemma. If they attacked the caravan now, they would be killing in a sacred month. Luckily, the sacred month ended today and tomorrow there would be no taboo about killing. But there was another problem. By tonight they would be in the sacred area of Mecca. In the sanctified area, there could never be any killing. They hesitated and talked about what to do. They decided to go ahead and kill as many as possible today and take their goods.

1425 Islam drew first blood and attacked the unarmed men. Amr was killed by an arrow. He was the first man to be killed in jihad. One man escaped and they captured two prisoners. They took their camels with their goods and headed back to Mohammed in Medina. On the way they talked about how Mohammed would get one fifth of the stolen goods, spoils.

1425 When they got back, Mohammed said that he did not order them to attack in the sacred month. So he held the caravan and the two prisoners in suspense and refused to do anything with the goods or prisoners. The prisoners said, "Mohammed has violated the sacred month, shed blood therein, stolen goods and taken prisoners." But the Koran said:

> 2:216 *You are commanded to fight although you dislike it. You may hate something that is good for you, and love something that is bad for you. Allah knows and you do not. When they ask you about fighting in the holy month, say: Fighting at this time is a serious offense, but it is worse in Allah's eyes to deny others the path to Him, to disbelieve in Him, and to drive His worshippers out of the Sacred Mosque. Idolatry is a greater sin than murder.*

1426 Exiling Mohammed from Mecca was worse than killing. To resist Islam was worse than murder. The spoils were distributed and a ransom set for the prisoners. The men who had killed and stolen were now concerned as to whether they would get their take of the spoils. So once again the Koran spoke:

> 2:218 *Those that have embraced the Faith, and those that have fled their land and fought for the cause of Allah, may hope for Allah's mercy. Allah is forgiving and merciful.*

FIGHTING IN ALLAH'S CAUSE—BADR

1428 Mohammed heard that Abu Sufyan was coming with a large caravan of thirty to forty Quraysh from Syria. Mohammed called the Muslims together and said, "Go out and attack it, perhaps Allah will give us the prey."

I428 As the caravan approached Medina, Abu Sufyan became worried and questioned every rider on the road about Mohammed. Then he heard intelligence that indeed Mohammed was going to attack. He sent out a fast rider to Mecca for aid.

I433 Mohammed and his men headed out of Medina for what was to prove to be one of the most important battles in all of history, a battle that would change the world forever.

I435 Mohammed was cheered. He said, "I see the enemy dead on the ground." They headed towards Badr where they camped near there for the night. He sent several scouts to the well at Badr and the scouts found two slaves with water camels. They felt sure they were from the Quraysh caravan and brought back them back to Mohammed. Two of Mohammed's men questioned them as Mohammed was nearby praying. The men replied that they were from the Quraysh. Mohammed's men began to beat them and torture the slaves as Mohammed prayed.

I436 Mohammed told his men that the slaves told them the truth until they started to beat and torture them. Then the slaves had lied but it had been the lie that they wanted to hear. Mohammed asked the men how many of the Quraysh there were and who were the leaders of the Quraysh. When they told him he was delighted and told his warriors that Mecca had sent their best men to be slaughtered.

I439-440 Both armies had an idea of the location of the other. Mohammed went ahead to chose a place to camp and set up for battle on the morrow.

I440-444 The Quraysh marched forth at daybreak. The battle started.

I445 Some arrows flew and one Muslim was killed. Mohammed addressed his army. "By Allah, every man who is slain this day by fighting with courage and advancing, not retreating, will enter Paradise." One of his men had been eating dates said, "You mean that there is nothing between me and Paradise except being killed by the Quraysh?" He flung the dates to the side, picked up his sword and set out to fight. He got his wish and was killed later.

I445 One of Mohammed's men asked what makes Allah laugh? Mohammed answered, "When he plunges into the midst of the enemy without armor." The man removed his coat of mail, picked up his sword and made ready to attack.

I445 Now the two armies started to close ranks and move forward. Mohammed had said that his warriors were not to start until he gave the order.

Now he took a handful of pebbles and threw them at the Quraysh and said, "Curse those faces." The Muslims advanced. The battle had begun.

I451 As the battle wound down, Mohammed issued orders for the fighters to be on the look out for Abu Jahl, the enemy of Allah, among the slain. He was found still fighting in a thicket. A Muslim made for him and cut off his lower leg. Another Muslim passed by him as Abu Jahl lay dying and put his foot on his neck and cut off his head.

I452 He took the head back to Mohammed and said, "Here is the head of the enemy of Allah" and threw it at Mohammed's feet. The Prophet said, "Praise be to Allah."

I455 As the bodies were dragged to a well, one of the Muslims saw the body of his father thrown in. He said, "My father was a virtuous, wise, kind, and cultured man. I had hoped he would become a Muslim. He died a Kafir." His abode is hellfire forever. [Before Islam killing of kin and tribal brothers had been forbidden since the dawn of time. After Islam brother would kill brother and sons would kill their fathers. Fighting in Allah's cause—jihad.]

I454 The bodies of the Quraysh were thrown into a well. The Apostle of Allah leaned over the well and shouted at the bodies, "Oh people of the well, have you found what Allah promised to be true?" The Muslims were puzzled by his question. Mohammed explained that the dead could hear him.

I456 Now it was time to take the property from the dead who could no longer claim what had been theirs. It was now the spoils of jihad and the profit of Islam. Mohammed divided it equally among all who were there. He took one fifth for himself.

I459 Off they set for Medina with the spoils of war and the prisoners to be ransomed. Except for one prisoner, who had spoken against Mohammed. He was brought in front of the Prophet to be killed and before the sword struck, he asked, "Who will care for my family?"

M230 The Prophet replied, "Hell!" After he fell dead, Mohammed said, "Unbeliever in Allah and his Prophet and his Book! I give thanks to Allah who has killed you and made my eyes satisfied."

This is the Sunna of Mohammed

JIHAD, THE JEWS' EXILE

CHAPTER 8

*61:11 Believe in Allah and His messenger and fight valiantly
for Allah's cause [jihad] with both your wealth and your
lives. It would be better for you, if you only knew it!*

SUMMARY

Mohammed now challenged the first of the three Jewish tribes to convert to Islam. They refused his offer. Soon he attacked the first Jewish tribe and won. Mohammed took all of their wealth and exiled them.

Mohammed continued his profitable jihad against the Meccan caravans.

Mohammed ordered his first assassination, against a Jew who wrote poems about him. He then ordered the murder of other Jews.

THE AFFAIR OF THE JEWS OF QAYNUQA

In Mecca, Mohammed had divided the community into those who followed Islam and those of the native Arabic religions. In Mecca he adopted all the classical Jewish stories to prove his prophesy and spoke well of the Jews. But there were almost no Jews living in Mecca, and therefore, no one to differ with him.

In Medina half of the population were Jews, who let Mohammed know that they disagreed with him. So in Medina, Mohammed argued with Jews as well as the Kafir Arabs. Even though there were very few in the town who were Christian, Mohammed argued against them as well. All Kafirs were verbally attacked in Medina.

I545 There were three tribes of Jews in Medina. The Beni Qaynuqa were gold smiths and lived in a stronghold in their quarters. It is said by Mohammed that they broke the treaty that had been signed when Mohammed came to Medina. How they did this is unclear.

I545 Mohammed assembled the Jews in their market and said: "Oh Jews, be careful that Allah does not bring vengeance upon you like what happened to the Quraysh. Become Muslims. You know that I am the prophet that was sent you. You will find that in your scriptures."

1545 They replied: "Oh Mohammed you seem to think that we are your people. Don't fool yourself. You may have killed and beaten a few merchants of the Quraysh, but we are men of war and real men."

1546 Some time later Mohammed besieged the Jews in the their quarters. None of the other two Jewish tribes came to their support. Finally the Jews surrendered and expected to be slaughtered after their capture.

1546 But an Arab ally bound to them by a client relationship approached Mohammed and said, "Oh Mohammed deal kindly with my clients." Mohammed ignored him. The ally repeated the request and again Mohammed ignored him. The ally grabbed Mohammed by the robe and enraged Mohammed who said, "Let me go!" The ally said, "No, you must deal kindly with my clients. They have protected me and now you would kill them all? I fear these changes." The response by the Koran:

> 5:51 *Oh, believers, do not take the Jews or Christians as friends. They are but one another's friends. If any one of you take them for his friends, he surely is one of them. Allah will not guide the evildoers.*
> 5:52 *You will see those who have a diseased heart race towards them and say, "We fear in case a change of fortune befalls us." Perhaps Allah will bring about some victory or event of His own order. Then they will repent of the thoughts they secretly held in their hearts.*

Mohammed exiled the Jews and took all of their wealth and goods.

THE RAID TO AL QARADA

1547 Mohammed's victory at Badr and ongoing jihad caused the Quraysh to go a different route to Syria. They hired a new guide to take them over the new route. Mohammed had intelligence about their route and sent a party to raid them. They were carrying a great deal of silver when the caravan stopped at a watering hole. The Muslims surprised them and the Quraysh managed to escape but Mohammed's men were able to steal all the caravan's goods, including the silver. The stolen goods were delivered to Mohammed in Medina.

THE ASSASSINATION OF AL ASHRAF, THE JEW

1548 When Al Ashraf, a Jew of Medina, heard that two of his friends had been killed at Badr, he said that the grave was a better place than the earth with Mohammed. So the "enemy of Allah" composed some poems bewailing the loss of his friends and attacking Islam.

1551 When Mohammed heard of Al Ashraf's criticism of his politics, he said, "Who will rid me of Al Ashraf?" A Muslim said, "I will kill him for you." Days later Mohammed found out that his assassin was not doing anything, including eating or drinking. Mohammed summoned him and asked what was going on. The man replied that he had taken on a task that was too difficult for him to do. Mohammed said that it was a duty which he should try to do. The assassin said, "Oh Apostle of Allah, I will have to tell a lie." The Prophet said, "Say what you like, you are free in the matter."

I552 By the use of lies three Muslims were able to kill Al Ashraf. When they returned to Mohammed, he was praying. They told him that they had killed the enemy of Allah. Their attack terrorized all the Jews. There was no Jew in Medina who was not afraid.

KILL ANY JEW THAT FALLS INTO YOUR POWER

I554 The Apostle of Allah said, "Kill any Jew who falls into your power." Hearing this Muhayyisa fell upon a Jewish merchant who was a business associate and killed him. His brother was not a Muslim and asked him how he could kill a man who had been his friend and partner in many business deals. The Muslim said that if Mohammed had asked him to kill his brother he would have done it immediately. His brother said, "You mean that if Mohammed said to cut off my head you would do it?" "Yes," was the reply. The older brother then said, "By Allah, any religion which bring you to this is marvelous." And he decided then and there to become a Muslim.

This is the Sunna of Mohammed

JIHAD, A SETBACK

CHAPTER 9

4:14 But those who disobey Allah and His Messenger
and go beyond His limits, will be led into the Fire to
live forever, and it will be a humiliating torment!

SUMMARY

The Meccans came to Medina with an army to seek revenge against their declared enemy, Mohammed. Mohammed decided to leave the security of the Medinan walls and meet in the field of battle.

At first the Muslims prevailed, but their greed about the spoils caused them to break ranks and lose to the Medinans.

The battle was important for Islam. It showed that Muslims must never vary from Mohammed's orders. Allah may be on the side of Islam, but Muslims must never falter. Of course, all of the slain Muslims warriors went to Paradise.

There would be more battles. Muslims must learn from their losses. Mohammed sent our assassins against one of his enemies.

THE BATTLE OF UHUD

I555 Back at Mecca those who had lost at the battle of Badr told others, "Men of Quraysh, Mohammed has killed your best men. Give us money so that we may take revenge." Money was raised, men were hired. An army was put together.

I558 So the Meccans camped near Medina, ready for war. Ready for revenge. The Muslims now needed a strategy. Many, including Mohammed, wanted to sit and let the Meccans attack Medina. The town itself could be used in a defensive way—walls and rooftops would give any defender a strong advantage. But blood ran hot with the Muslims warriors. The arguments went on until Mohammed went in his house and came out in his armor.

I559 Mohammed said, "When a prophet puts on his armor, he should not take it off until there has been war." So he marched out with a 1000 men to meet the Meccans.

I560 When they saw the Meccans, Mohammed said, "Let there be no fighting until I give the word." Mohammed placed 50 archers to protect his rear and flank. They must not move but hold that ground. Mohammed put on a second coat of mail.

I570 The Muslims fought without fear and the battle went against the Meccans who were cut off from their camp that had the spoils of war. The Muslim archers left their positions to get to the spoils. The battle might go to Islam, but the treasure would be theirs. This left the flank and rear open and the Meccan cavalry took advantage and charged the rear where Mohammed was. The battle suddenly went against the Muslims.

I571 The Muslims were put to flight and many were slain. Even Mohammed got hit in the face by a rock, broke a tooth and split his lip. He was incensed.

I574 Mohammed fled the field. He was a heavy man, and wore two suits of armor. He almost could not climb the rocks and hill without help.

I583 The day went to the Meccans, the Quraysh. The Meccans did not press their advantage. They came to extract tribal justice and they killed about as many the Muslims had killed at Badr.

I586 The dead Muslims were buried in the battlefield. Mohammed said, "I testify that none who are wounded in jihad but what he will be raised by Allah with his bleeding wounds smelling like the finest perfume."

I587 When Mohammed entered his house he handed his sword to his daughter and told her, "Wash the blood from this for by Allah it has served me well today."

Since Allah had sent angels to the previous battle of Badr and the outnumbered Muslims triumphed, how could they fail at Uhud?

I597 The reason that Allah let the Meccans win was to test the Muslims. Now they will know their true selves. If they obey Mohammed, then they can become true Muslims. A true Muslim never loses his morale, never falls into despair.

ASSASSINATION AS JIHAD

M276 After Uhud, several tribes allied themselves under the leadership of Sufyan Ibn Khalid. Mohammed dispatched an assassin to kill him. The assassin, Abdullah, joined his forces and waited until he was alone with him. He killed Sufyan and beheaded him and went back to Medina.

M276 Abdullah then went straight to Mohammed and presented Mohammed with the head of his enemy. Mohammed was gratified and presented him with his walking stick. He said, "This is a token between you and me on the Day of Resurrection. Very few will have such to lean on in that day." Abdullah attached it to his sword scabbard.

THE RAID ON THE MUSTALIQ TRIBE

I725 When Mohammed heard that the Arab tribe, the Mustaliq, were opposed to him and were gathering against him, he set out with his army to attack them. Islam was victorious and the Mustaliq and their women, children, and goods were taken as spoils of war.

I729 The captives of the tribe of Mustaliq were parceled out as spoils with a ransom price. If the ransom were not paid then the people were treated as spoils and slaves. Now one of them was a beautiful woman with a high price on her. Mohammed paid the ransom for the beautiful woman and she would become his wife. Now in spite of the fact that she was already married, there was no problem. It was a deal. Mohammed paid the ransom and the beautiful woman became wife number seven.

I729 This marriage had a side effect. The captives were now related to Mohammed's wife. They were all released without ransom.

THE DEATH OF A POETESS

I996 There was a poetess who wrote a poem against Islam. Mohammed said, "Who will rid me of Marwan's daughter?" One of his followers heard him and on that very night he went to the woman's home to kill her.

M239 The assassin was able to do the work in the dark as the woman slept. Her other children lay in the room, but her babe lay on her breast. The stealthy assassin removed the child and drove the knife into her with such force that he pined her to the bed.

I996 In the morning he went to Mohammed and told him. Mohammed said, "You have helped Allah and his Apostle."

M239 Mohammed turned to the people in the mosque, he said, "If you wish to see a man who has assisted Allah and his Prophet, look here." Omar cried, "What, the blind Omeir!" "No," said Mohammed, "call him Omeir the Seeing."

I996 The poetess had five sons and the assassin went to them and said, "I killed Bint Marwan, Oh sons. Withstand me if you can; don't keep me waiting." Islam became powerful that day and many became Muslims when they saw the power of Islam.

This is the Sunna of Mohammed

JIHAD, THE JEWS SUBMIT

CHAPTER 10

*58:20 Those who oppose Allah and His Messenger will be laid
low. Allah has declared, "Surely I will be victorious, along
with My messengers." Truly Allah is strong and mighty.*

SUMMARY

Mohammed attacked the second of the three Jewish tribes who
were in Medina. They were date farmers and he burned their plan-
tations. They surrendered and Mohammed took all of their wealth
and drove them from the town

The Meccans returned with an army to attack Mohammed. But
he installed a trench (a unique strategy in Arabia) and foiled their
plans. Mohammed used both spies and secret agents to work behind
the scenes and weaken the Meccan alliances.

CLEANSING

1652 It had been four years since Mohammed came to Medina. Mohammed went to one of the two remaining Jewish tribes to ask for blood
money for the two men his fighter had killed. At first they said yes, but
as they talked about it they decided that this would be a good time to kill
Mohammed. Here he was in their quarter of Medina sitting on a wall near
a roof. Why not send a man up and drop a rock on this man who had been
such a sorrow to them? Mohammed got word of the plot and left.

1653 This was as good a reason as any to deal with the Jews. The same
Jews who insisted that he was not the prophet. He raised his army and
went off to put their fortresses under siege. These Jews were farmers and
they grew the finest dates in all of Arabia. So Mohammed cut and burned
their date palms as they watched. They called out, "You have prohibited
wanton destruction and blamed those who do that. Now you do what you
forbid."

1653 Now the other Jewish tribe had assured them that they would
come to their defense. But no Jew would stand with another Jew against
Islam. With no help from their brothers, the besieged Jews cut a deal with

the apostle of Allah. Spare their lives and let them go with what they could carry on their camels, except for their armor.

1654 When there was fighting in jihad, the fighter got four-fifths. But since there had been no fighting there was no reason to give four-fifths to the jihadists. All of the spoils went to Mohammed, not just one fifth.

1654 There were some new problems created—the burning of the date palms and all the money going to Mohammed. The Koran had the answers. It was Allah who wrecked his vengeance upon the Jews and gave Mohammed power over them. It was even Allah who caused the Jews to tear down their own houses.

> 59:2 It was He who caused the People of the Book [the Jews] to leave their homes and go into the first exile. They did not think they would leave, and they thought that their fortresses could protect them from Allah. But Allah's wrath reached them from where they did not expect it and cast terror into their hearts, so that they destroyed their homes with their own hands, as well as by the hands of the believers.

1654 And the Jews were very fortunate that Allah let them go with a few worldly processions. They got out alive, Allah did not slay them, but they will burn in Hell since they resisted Mohammed. As far as the wanton destruction of the palm trees can not be laid to Mohammed, it was the Jew's fault.

> 59:3 And if Allah had not decreed their exile, surely He would have punished them in this world. And in the world to come they will receive the punishment of the Fire because they had disobeyed Allah and His Messenger. Whoever disobeys Allah, knows that Allah is truly severe in His punishment.
>
> 59:5 Allah gave you permission to cut down some palm trees and leave others intact so as to shame the wicked [the Jews]. After Allah gave the spoils to His Messenger, you made no move with horses or camels to capture them [the Jews], but Allah gives His messengers power over what He chooses. Allah is all-powerful.

THE BATTLE OF THE TRENCH

1669 Some of the Jews who had been exiled from Medina decided that they needed to destroy Mohammed and to do that they needed allies. Since allies were to be found in Mecca, they went there and parlayed with the leaders of the Quraysh. But since this was a war of religion, the Quraysh wanted was proof of religious supremacy to Mohammed. So the leaders said to the Jews, "You are People of the Book and you know our disagreement. Who has the better religion, us or Mohammed?" The leaders of the Jews replied that the Quraysh had the better religion.

I669 Now the Koran could not pass up such an insult to Mohammed. So the Koran says:

> 4:49 *Have you not seen those who praise themselves for their purity? But Allah purifies whom He pleases, and they will not be treated unjustly in the slightest degree. See how they make up lies about Allah! That in itself is a terrible sin. Have you not seen those [Jews allied with the Meccans] to whom part of the Scriptures were given? They believe in idols and sorcery, and they say of the Kafirs, "These are guided on a better path than the believers." It is on these whom Allah has laid His curse. Those who are cursed by Allah will have no one to help them.*

I669-670 So the Meccans entered into an alliance with the Jews. Another Arab tribe joined the alliance as well.

As Mohammed had many spies in Mecca, so it took no time until he knew of the coming fight and he set out to prepare for it. There was a Persian who suggested to Mohammed that he build a trench as a barrier against the Meccans and their allies. For eight days the Arabs worked at building a trench, or ditch, around the weak points of Medina. To help with morale Mohammed personally pitched in and did his turn at manual labor.

I673 But the work was done just in time. The Quraysh and the other allies camped near the trench. Mohammed and his army camped on their side of the trench and sent the women and children to the forts.

I674 One of the exiled Jews approached the last tribe of Jews in Medina to be allies with the attacking Meccans. At first the Jews would not even talk to him. After all, if Mohammed won, they would be left with the consequences of dealing with a man who had driven the other two tribes of Jews from Medina. But in the end the Jews agreed to lend aid if the battle started to go against Mohammed.

I677-683 Mohammed was able to use his agents to sow discord among those allied against him. The trench defense frustrated the Meccans. The weather was bad and the allies were distrustful of each other. In terms of actual combat only a handful of men were killed over the twenty-day siege. The Meccans broke camp and went back home. It was a victory for Mohammed.

This is the Sunna of Mohammed

JIHAD, THE JEWS AGAIN

CHAPTER 11

58:5 Those who oppose Allah and His Messenger will
be laid low, just as those who came before them.

SUMMARY

Gabriel commanded Mohammed to attack the Jews of Medina. The Muslim troops put the Jews under siege. They surrendered after 25 days. The women and children were enslaved. All 800 adult, male Jews were beheaded. All of their goods were taken as booty.

Mohammed then had a Jewish leader assassinated.

THE SOLUTION FOR THE JEWS

1684 That same day the angel Gabriel came to Mohammed at noon. He asked if Mohammed were through fighting. Gabriel and the angels were going to attack the last Jewish tribe in Medina, the Banu Qurayza. Gabriel said, "Allah commands you to go to the Jews. I am headed there now to shake their stronghold."

1684 So Mohammed called upon his troops and they headed to the forts of the Jews. Now the B. Qurayza of Medina lived in forts that were on the outskirts of Medina. Mohammed rode up to the forts and called out, "You brothers of apes, has Allah disgraced you and brought His vengeance upon you?"

1685-689 Mohammed put the Jews under siege for twenty-five days. Finally, the Jews offered to submit their fate to a Muslim, Saed, with whom they had been an ally in the past. His judgment was simple. Kill all the men. Take their property and take the women and children as captives. Mohammed said, "You have given the judgment of Allah."

1690 The captives were taken into Medina. They dug trenches in the market place of Medina. It was a long day, but 800 Jews met their death that day. Mohammed and his twelve year old wife sat and watched the entire day and into the night. The Apostle of Allah had every male Jew killed.

1693 Mohammed took the property, wives and children of the Jews, and divided it up amongst the Muslims. Mohammed took his one fifth of the slaves and sent a Muslim with the female Jewish slaves to a nearby city where the women were sold for pleasure. Mohammed invested the money from the sale of the female slaves for horses and weapons.

1693 There was one last piece of spoils for Mohammed. The most beautiful Jewess was his slave for pleasure.

1696-7 In the battle of the Trench it was Allah who had won the day. Allah is what gives the Muslim his strength and will. No matter what the Kafirs do Allah will triumph.

> 33:25 *And Allah drove back the Kafirs in their wrath, and they gained nothing by it. Allah aided the believers in the war, for Allah is strong and mighty. He brought down some of the People of the Book [the Jews] out of their fortresses to aid the confederates and to strike terror into their hearts. Some you killed, and others you took captive. He made you heirs of their land, their homes, and their possessions, and even gave you another land on which you had never before set foot.*

THE KILLING OF THE JEW, SALLAM

1714-6 A Jew named Sallam helped to plan and organize the confederation of the tribes that attacked Mohammed in the Battle of the Trench. Mohammed sent five Muslim men to assassinate Sallam. When the men had done their work, they returned to Mohammed and fell to arguing as to who actually killed Sallam. Mohammed demanded to see their swords. He examined them one by one and then pointed to the sword that had been the killing weapon. It had food on it still from the thrust to the stomach.

The Koran's last words about the Jews:

> 5:13 *Because they [the Jews] broke their covenant, We have cursed them and have hardened their hearts. They change words from their places and have forgotten part of what they were taught. You will always discover them in deceits, except for a few of them, but forgive them and overlook their misdeeds. Allah loves those who act generously.*

> 5:42 *They [the Jews] are fond of listening to lies or devouring anything forbidden. If they do come to you [Mohammed], judge between them, or refuse to interfere. If you withdraw from them, they cannot harm you in any way, but if you judge, then judge between them with equity. Allah loves those who deal equitably. Why would they make you their judge since they possess their own law, the Torah, which holds the commands of Allah, yet they have not obeyed it? These are not believers.*

This is the Sunna of Mohammed

THE TREATY OF AL HUDAYBIYA

CHAPTER 12

*4:136 Believers! Believe in Allah and His Messenger
and in the Scriptures which were sent down to His
Messenger and in the Scriptures He sent down before him.
Those who deny Allah, His angels, His Scriptures, His
messengers, and the Last Day have gone far astray.*

SUMMARY

Mohammed wanted to go to Mecca for a pilgrimage, but Mecca was filled with enemies. He went anyway, and the Meccans sent out a delegation to prevent his entry.

The Meccans then negotiated a treaty with Mohammed. The Muslims thought this to be a loss, but Mohammed and the Koran pointed out that Islam had now been recognized as a political power, and jihad would start again when Islam grew stronger. The treaty was only temporary and gave Islam time to grow stronger.

1740 Mohammed decided to make a pilgrimage to Mecca. A difficult problem was how to do this peacefully. The state of affairs between Mohammed and the Meccans had always condemnation and violence. He called for all to go, but the Bedouin Arabs from around Medina refused his call. So he headed out with 700 men and 70 sacrificial camels. He and the others wore the white garments of the pilgrims so that the Meccans would not suspect jihad.

1741 As they approached Mecca, he found out that the Quraysh had come out prepared for war and were blocking the way. So Mohammed took an alternate and difficult route to Mecca and try to avoid the armed Meccans.

1743 The Meccans were not going to let him enter, war or no war. They would not submit to Mohammed's wishes. They would not lose face with the other Arabs.

1747 The Meccans set a man out to parlay and make a treaty with Mohammed. Umar was furious that Mohammed would even make a treaty with Kafirs. To make a treaty with Kafirs was demeaning to Islam. But Mohammed told him that Allah would not make them the loser. They would win over the Quraysh. Be patient.

1747 So they drew up a treaty to the effect that there would be no war for ten years, there would be no hostilities, no one could convert to Islam without their guardians' permission. In turn the Muslims could come next year and stay for three days in Mecca, but they could not enter this year.

1748 Many of the Muslims were depressed. Mohammed had promised that they could enter Mecca. Now they could not. Before they left they sacrificed the camels and shaved their heads doing as much of the rituals they could without getting into Mecca.

1749 On the way back to Medina, Mohammed added to the Koran, the sura called Victory about this treaty. Those who held back [the desert Arabs, Bedouins] and did not come on the pilgrimage would not profit by getting any spoils of war. And there is more war in the future.

> 48:15 *Those who lagged behind will say, when you go to take the spoils of war, "Let us follow you." They wish to change the word [the rules of how to divide the spoils of war] of Allah. Say: You will not follow us. Allah has already declared this. They will say, "No, you are jealous of us." No, they understand little. Say to those desert Arabs who were left behind, "You will be called to fight against a people of mighty strength. You will fight until they submit. If you obey, Allah will give you a goodly reward, but if you turn back, as you turned back before, He will punish you with a grievous penalty.*

1750 This was a victory for Islam. The government of Mecca dealt with Mohammed as an independent political power. Many more Arabs were attracted to Islam with its new power.

1754 The treaty greatly enhanced the Islam's power. Part of the treaty was that those who had become Muslims without the permission of their guardians would be returned to the Quraysh. But some of the women wished to stay and not return. The Koran ruled that their dowries be returned and the women could stay.

This is the Sunna of Mohammed

JIHAD, THE FIRST DHIMMIS

CHAPTER 13

4:80 Those who obey the Messenger, obey Allah. As for those who turn away from you, We have not sent you to watch over them.

SUMMARY

Mohammed now had a treaty with the Meccans and he turned his attention the Jews who lived in Khaybar, a town two days from Medina.

Mohammed captured the Jewish forts and signed a treaty with the Jews so that they became semi-slaves called *dhimmis*. The Jews would work the land and give half of the profits to Mohammed.

He took their wealth and took the most beautiful Jewess as his wife.

The Jews of Fadak panicked and surrendered to become dhimmis and gave Mohammed their wealth.

KHAYBAR

I756 After the treaty of Al Hudaybiya, Mohammed stayed in Medina for about two months before he collected his army and marched to the forts of Khaybar, a community of wealthy Jewish farmers who lived in a village of separate forts about 100 miles from Medina.

I758 Mohammed seized the forts one at a time. Among the captives was a beautiful Jewess named Safiya whose husband had been slain by Mohammed when she was still a newlywed. In addition, he had her father tortured to death and killed her cousin. Mohammed took her for his sexual pleasure. One of his men had first chosen her for his own slave of pleasure, but Mohammed traded him two of her cousins for Safiya. Mohammed always got first choice of the spoils of war and the women.

> Bukhari5,59,512 *During the night, just outside Khaybar, Mohammed gave the Fajr Prayer and said, "Allah is great! Khaybar will be in ruins. When we attack a city that has been warned, those people are in for an evil morning." As the people of Khaybar fled the city, Mohammed ordered the men killed and the women and children enslaved.*

47

I759 On the occasion of Khaybar, Mohammed put forth new orders about the sex with captive women. If the woman was pregnant, she was not to be used for sex until after the birth of the child. Nor were any women to be used for sex who were unclean with regards to the Muslim laws about menstruation.

1764 Mohammed knew that there was a large treasure hidden somewhere in Khaybar, so he brought forth the Jew who he thought knew the most about it and questioned him. The Jew denied any knowledge. Mohammed told one of his men, "Torture the Jew until you extract what he has." So the Jew was staked on the ground, and a small fire built on his chest to get him to talk. When the man was nearly dead and still would not talk, Mohammed had him released and taken to one of his men who had a brother killed in the fight. This Muslim got the pleasure of cutting off the tortured Jew's head.

1764 At Khaybar Mohammed instituted the first dhimmis. After the best of the goods were taken from the Jews Mohammed left them to work the land. Since his men knew nothing about farming, and the Jews were skilled at it, they worked the land and gave Mohammed half of their profits.

> Bukhari3,39,521 *Mohammed made an agreement with the Jews of Khaybar that allowed them to use the land in exchange for half of each harvest. ..*

1774 There were a total of 1,800 people who divided up the wealth taken from the beaten Jews of Khaybar. A cavalry man got three shares, a foot soldier got one share. Mohammed appointed eighteen chiefs to divide the loot. Mohammed received his one-fifth before it was distributed.

FADAK

I777 The Jews of Fadak panicked when they saw what Mohammed did at Khaybar. They would be next, so they surrendered to Mohammed without a fight. Since there was no battle Mohammed got 100% of their goods and they worked the land and gave half to Mohammed each year. They became dhimmis like those of Khaybar.

This is the Sunna of Mohammed

MOHAMMED'S FINAL JIHAD

CHAPTER 14

3:53 "Our Lord! We believe in what Thou hast
revealed, and we follow the Apostle; then write
us down among those who bear witness."

SUMMARY

A year after his treaty with the Meccans, the Muslims went on their pilgrimage to Mecca.

The Muslims lost the battle at Muta against a Christian army.

Mohammed used a minor event to cancel his treaty and send an army to conquer Mecca.

Mohammed entered Mecca, took political control, destroyed all art and issued death warrants against every artist and opponent.

Mohammed's last jihad to Tabuk did not go well as many Muslims did not want to go on the difficult campaign.

The Koran spoke at length condemning Muslims who do not follow the command for jihad. Jihad is eternal and for all Muslims.

THE PILGRIMAGE

1789 After returning from Khaybar, Mohammed sent out many raiding parties and expeditions. Seven years after Mohammed moved to Medina and one year after the treaty of Hudaybiya, Mohammed led the Muslims to the Kabah in Mecca.

1790 After his three day stay in Mecca, the Quraysh asked him to leave as per the treaty. Mohammed asked to stay and have a wedding feast and he would invite the Quraysh. The Quraysh said no, please leave. He left.

THE RAID ON MUTA

1791-3 Mohammed sent an army of 3000 to Muta soon after his return from Mecca. Now Muta was north of Medina, near Syria. When they arrived the Muslims found a large army of the Byzantine Christians.

1796 The Muslims were cut to ribbons. The Byzantines were professionals and superior in numbers.

1798 The Muslims who remained behind in Medina scorned the returning fighters. They threw dirt at them and said, "You are runaways. You fled from the way of Allah. You fled from jihad." Poetry was written to the effect that the men kept their distance from the Byzantine army and were afraid of death. They loved life too much and feared death.

MECCA CONQUERED

1803 At the treaty of Hudaybiya, it was agreed that the Meccans and Mohammed could make alliances between themselves and other tribes. A small violation of the treaty allowed Mohammed to end it and march on Mecca with 10,000 men to punish them.

1813-4 The chief of the Meccans, Abu Sufyan, came to the Muslim camp to negotiate. Mohammed said, "Abu Sufyan, submit and testify that there is no god but Allah and that Mohammed is his apostle before you lose your head!" So he submitted.

Abu Sufyan went ahead and announced to Mecca that Mohammed's army was coming. They were not to resist but to go into their houses, his house or the Kabah and that they would be safe.

1819 Mohammed had told his commanders only to kill those who resisted. Otherwise they were to bother no one except for those who had spoken against Mohammed. The list of those to be killed:

- One of Mohammed's secretaries, who had said that when he was recording Mohammed's Koranic revelations sometimes Mohammed let the secretary insert better speech. This caused him to lose faith and he became an apostate.
- Two singing girls who had sung satires against Mohammed.
- A Muslim tax collector who had become an apostate (left Islam).
- A man who had insulted Mohammed.

1821 Mohammed went to the Kabah and rode around it seven times. Each time he went past the Black Stone, he touched it with his stick. Then he called for the key to the Kabah and entered. There was a wooden dove carved that he picked up and broke and threw out the door. There were 360 ritual objects representing the gods of the various Arab faiths. Mohammed had them all destroyed by burning.

Mohammed announced the end of all feuds, all revenge killings, payment of blood money. Veneration of the ancestors was over.

THE BATTLE OF HUNAIN

1840 When Mohammed took Mecca, the surrounding Arab tribes saw that if he was not opposed he would be King of Arabia. The Hawazin Arabs decided to oppose him under the leadership of Malik.

1842 Mohammed sent a spy to gather intelligence about the Arabs. When he received the information, he set about for jihad.

1845 When the army descended into the broad area, they found the enemy prepared and hiding, waiting to attack. The Muslim troops broke and ran. Mohammed stood in his stirrups and called out, "Where are you going? Come to me, the Apostle of Allah." Most of the men continued to retreat except his battle hardened core troops who regrouped around him. About a core of 100 lead the charge to turn the tide. They were steadfast. Mohammed looked at the carnage and said, "Now the oven is hot!" Islam triumphed again.

THE RAID ON TABUK

1894 Mohammed decided to raid the Byzantine Christians. The men began to prepare, but with no enthusiasm due to the heat, it was time for harvest to begin and they remembered the last combat with the Byzantines—they lost badly.

1896 So Mohammed set off, but there were many Muslims who were slow to leave or they came with misgivings. After the first camp some of the Muslims left and returned to Medina. These were called hypocrites.

1902 When they got to Tabuk, the Christian dhimmis there paid the poll tax, *jizya*. By paying the poll tax, a per person tax, they would not be attacked, killed or robbed by the Muslims. Those who paid the jizya were under the protection of Islam

1903 Mohammed sent Khalid to the fort of a Christian chief. When the chief and his brother rode out of their fort to inspect the cattle, Khalid killed the chief's brother and captured the ruler. The chief to be a dhimmi and to pay the poll tax to Islam. Mohammed returned to Medina.

The Battle of Tabuk was hard for Mohammed. The Muslims did not come out to be jihadists as they had before. But the Koran makes clear that jihad is an obligation.

ETERNAL JIHAD

M448 After all the victories, some Muslims said that the days of fighting were over and even began to sell their arms. But Mohammed forbid this, saying, "There shall not cease from the midst of my people a party engaged in fighting for the truth, until the Antichrist appears." Jihad was recognized as the normal state of affairs. Indeed, the Koran prepares the way for this:

> 9:122 *The faithful should not all go out together to fight. If a part of every troop remained behind, they could instruct themselves in their religion and warn their people when they return to them that they should guard against evil.*
>
> 9:123 *Believers, fight the Kafirs who are near you, and let them find you to be tough and hard. Know that Allah is with those who guard against evil.*

1924 The Koran then turns to the issue of the raid on the Byzantine Christians at Tabuk. Muslims must answer the call to jihad. It is an obligation. If the Byzantine raid had been short and had made for easy war spoils, the Muslims would have joined readily. But instead they made excuses. A Muslim's duty is not to avoid fighting with their person and money.

1926 Those who try to avoid jihad are hypocrites. The Prophet should struggle against them. They are bound for Hell.

> 9:73 *Oh, Prophet, strive hard against the Kafirs and the hypocrites, and be firm with them. Hell will be their dwelling place: A wretched journey.*

Those who believe in Allah and the Apostle and enter jihad with their wealth and selves will prosper and enter Paradise. This is a promise from Allah.

> 9:111 *Allah has bought from the believers their lives and their wealth, and in return, theirs is the Garden of Paradise. They will fight on the path of Allah so they slay and are slain.*

1933 When Mohammed had taken Mecca and Tabuk, deputations began to come from the Arabs. The Arabs were waiting to see what would happen between the Quraysh and Mohammed. When Mohammed was victorious, the Arabs came in groups and joined with him.

This is the Sunna of Mohammed

THE CHRISTIANS

CHAPTER 15

33:21 You have an excellent example in Allah's Messenger
for those of you who put your hope in Allah and the
Last Day and who praise Allah continually.

SUMMARY

The Sira lays out the reasons that Jesus is only a Messenger of Allah. Kings ruled Jesus; he did not rule kings.

The Koran lays out the real Jesus. Jesus had no power, except what Allah gave him.

There is no Trinity. The purpose of Jesus was to give the message that Ahmed (Mohammed) would be coming.

Christians are members of the family of Abraham.

1404 While some Christians were in Medina, they argued religion with Mohammed. They held forth with the doctrine of the Trinity and the divinity of Christ. Mohammed later laid out the Islamic doctrine of the Christian doctrine. The Koran tells in detail the real story of Jesus, who is just another of Allah's prophets, and that the Trinity of the Christians is Allah, Jesus and Mary.

1406 No one has power except through Allah. Allah gave the prophet Jesus the power of raising the dead, healing the sick, making birds of clay and having them fly away. Allah gave Jesus these signs as a mark of his being a prophet. But Allah did not give the powers of appointing kings, the ability to change night to day. These lacks of power show that Jesus was a man, not part of a Trinity. If he were part of God, then all powers would have been in his command. Then he would not have to have been under the dominion of kings.

> 3:20 *If they argue with you, then say: I have surrendered myself entirely to Allah, as have my followers. Say to the People of the Book and to the ignorant: "Do you surrender to Allah?" If they become Muslims, then they will be guided to the right path, but if they reject it, then your job is only to warn them. Allah watches over all His servants.*

3:21 *Warn those who do not believe in Allah's revelations, and who un-justly kill the messengers and those who teach justice, of the excruciating punishment they will receive. Their works will be meaningless in this world and in the world to come, and they will have no one to help them!*

3:23 *Consider those who have received part of the Scriptures. When they are called to accept the Book of Allah, some of them turn away and are op-posed to it. This is because they say, "We will only have to endure the Fire for a few days." They have created their own lies regarding their religion. How will they react when We gather them together on the assured day, and every soul will receive what it has earned, and they will not be dealt with unjustly?*

3:26 *Say: Allah! Lord of heaven and earth, you give power to whom you choose and take it away from whom you chose. You lift up whom you choose, and You bring down whom you choose. All that is good lies within your hand. You have power to do all things. You cause the night to turn into day, and the day to turn into night. You bring the living out of the dead, and the dead out of the living, and You give generously to whom you please.*

1407-8 Christ spoke in the cradle and then spoke to men as a grown man. Speaking from the cradle is a sign of his being a prophet. Christ's prophethood was confirmed by making clay birds fly. By Allah Christ healed the blind, the lepers, and raised the dead.

> 5:109 *One day Allah will assemble the messengers and say, "What response did you receive from mankind?" They will say, "We have no knowledge. You are the knower of secrets." Then Allah will say, "Oh Jesus, Son of Mary, remember my favor to you and your mother when I strengthened you with the Holy Spirit [Gabriel] so that you would speak to men alike in child-hood and when grown. I taught you the Scripture, wisdom, the Torah, and the Gospel, and you created the figure of a bird with clay, by my permis-sion, and breathed into it. With My permission it became a bird. You also healed the blind and the leper, with My permission. With My permission you raised the dead. I restrained the Children of Israel from harming you when you went to them with clear signs, and the unbelievers said, "This is nothing but plain sorcery."*
>
> 5:111 *When I revealed to the disciples, "Believe in Me and the One I sent," they said, "We believe and bear witness to You that we are Muslims."*

1408 Christ only comes through Allah. Christ's signs of being a proph-et come only from Allah. Jesus enjoins others to worship Allah, not him. But people refused to hear him, the Disciples came forth to help him with his mission. The Disciples were servants of Allah and were Muslims just like Christ.

3:44 This is one of the secret revelations revealed to you, Mohammed. You were not there when they cast their lots to see who would have guardianship of Mary, nor were you there when they argued about her. And remember when the angels said to Mary, "Allah brings you good news of His Word. His name will be Messiah, Jesus, Son of Mary, worthy of honor in this world and the world to come, one who is near to Allah. He will speak to the people when in the cradle and as a man. He will live a righteous life." She said, "My Lord! How can I have a son when no man has ever touched me?" He said, "It will be so. Allah creates what He will, and when He decrees a plan, all He must do is say, 'Be' and it is!" Allah will teach him the Scriptures and Wisdom, the Law, and the Gospel. He will be sent out as a messenger to the Children of Israel saying, "I have come to you with a sign from your Lord. I will make a figure of a bird out of clay and then, by Allah's will, I will breathe life into it. By Allah's permission I cause the blind to see, heal the lepers, and bring the dead back to life. I will tell you what you should eat and what you should store up in your houses. This will be a sign for those who truly believe. I have come to fulfill the Law which came before me and to give you permission to do certain things which were once unlawful. I come to you with a sign from your Lord, so fear Allah and obey me. Allah is my Lord and yours, so worship Him. That is the right path."

3:52 When Jesus saw that they did not believe, he said, "Who will be my helpers for Allah?" The disciples replied, "We will be Allah's helpers! We believe in Allah and witness our submission to Him. Lord! We believe in what you have revealed and we follow Your messenger; therefore, record us as Your witnesses."

1409 Christ was not crucified. When the Jews plotted against Christ, they found Allah to be the best plotter. Allah took Jesus up directly to him and will refute those who say he was crucified and was resurrected. On the final day, the Day of Resurrection, those who follow Christ but do not believe in his divinity will be blessed. Those who insist that Christ is God, part of the Trinity, and reject true faith will be punished in Hell.

3:54 So the Jews plotted and Allah plotted, but Allah is the best of plotters. And Allah said, "Jesus! I am going to end your life on earth and lift you up to Me. [Jesus did not die on the cross. He was taken to Allah. He will return to kill the anti-Christ and then die a natural death.] I will send the unbelievers away from you and lift up those who believe above all others until the Day of Resurrection. Then all will return to Me and I will judge their disputes. As for the unbelievers, they will be punished with excruciating agony in this world and the world to come. They will have no one to help them. As for the believers who do good works, He will fully reward

them. *Allah does not love those who do wrong. These signs and this wise warning We bring to you.*"
3:59 *Truly, Jesus is like Adam [neither had a father] in Allah's sight. He created him from the dust and said to him, "Be!" and he was.*

Although the Koran says less about Christians than Jews, it does address them.

4:171 *People of the Book [Christians]! Do not overstep the boundaries of your religion and speak only what is true about Allah. The Messiah, Jesus, the son of Mary, is only Allah's messenger and his Word which he sent into Mary was a spirit from Him. Therefore, believe in Allah and His messengers and do not say, "Trinity." Hold back and it will be better for you. Allah is only one god. Far be it from Allah to have a son! All in the heavens and earth are His. Allah is the sufficient as a protector. The Messiah does not condescend to be Allah's servant, nor do His favored angels. Those who disdain service to Him, and are filled with arrogance, Allah will gather them all together before Him.*

61:6 *And remember when Jesus, son of Mary, said, "Children of Israel! I am Allah's messenger sent to confirm the Law which was already revealed to you and to bring good news of a messenger who will come after me whose name will be Ahmad." [Ahmad was one of Mohammed's names. This quote of Jesus is not found in any Christian scriptures.] Yet when he [Mohammed] came to them with clear signs, they said, "This is merely sorcery!" And who is more evil than the one who, when called to submit to Islam, makes up a lie about Allah? Allah does not guide the evil-doers! They wish to put out Allah's light with their mouths, but as much as the unbelievers hate it, Allah will perfect His light.*
61:9 *It is He who has sent forth His messenger with guidance and the true religion so that, though the idolaters hate it, He will make His religion victorious over all the others.*

5:112 *Remember when the disciples said, "Oh Jesus, Son of Mary, is your Lord able to send down a table to us spread with food from heaven?" He said, "Fear Allah if you are believers." They said, "We desire to eat from it, to satisfy hearts, to know that you have spoken the truth to us, and to be witnesses to the miracle." Jesus, Son of Mary, said, "Oh Allah, our Lord, send down a table spread with food from heaven that it will become a recurring festival from the first of us and to the last of us, and a sign from You, and do nourish us, for You are the best provider." Allah said, "I will send it down to you, but whoever among you disbelieves after that, I will surely inflict a punishment on him unlike any I have inflicted on any other creature."*

5:116 *And when Allah says, "Oh Jesus, Son of Mary, did you say to mankind, 'Take me and my mother as two gods, beside Allah?'" He will say, "Glory be unto You. It is not for me to say what I had no right to say. If I had said that, You would have known it. You know what is in my heart. I do not know what is in Your heart. You know all that is hidden." "I only said what You commanded me to say, 'Worship Allah, my Lord and your Lord,' and I was a witness of their actions while I was among them. When You caused me to die, You watched them, and You are witness of all things. If You punish them, they are Your servants, and if You forgive them, You are mighty and wise."*

The Koran often uses the term People of the Book. At the time of Mohammed there were no books in Arabic. The written Arabic was used mostly for business. Since both Christianity and Judaism used religious texts this was distinctive. The term People of the Book can refer to either Jews, Christians, or both Jews and Christians. While in Medina Mohammed spoke of Allah's problems with the People of the Book.

3:64 *Say: People of the Book [Christians and Jews]! Let us settle upon an agreement: We will worship no one except Allah, we will set up no one as His equal, and none of us will take one from among us as a lord besides Allah. If they reject your proposal say, "Bear witness then that we are Muslims."*

3:65 *People of the Book! Why do you argue about Abraham [whether Abraham was a Jew or Christian] when the Law and the Gospel were not sent down until after him? Do you not understand? Listen, you are the ones who have argued about things of which you have some knowledge [arguments about Moses and Jesus], so then why do you argue about things of which you have no knowledge? Allah has knowledge, but you do not.*

THE FINAL STATE OF THE CHRISTIANS

CHAPTER 16

24:51 But when Allah and His Messenger call
the true believers to judge between them, their
response is, "We have heard, and we obey."

SUMMARY

Mohammed took his last pilgrimage to Mecca and gave his last sermon.

The final state of Christians and Jews is subservience to Islam.

After averaging a violent event every six weeks for nine years, Mohammed died.

THE FAREWELL PILGRIMAGE

1968 Ten years after entering Medina Mohammed made what was to be his last pilgrimage to Mecca. There he made his farewell address.

1969 The men have rights over their wives and the wives have rights over the men. The wives must never commit adultery nor act in a sexual manner towards others. If they do, put them in separate rooms and beat them lightly. If they refrain from these things, they have the right to food and clothing. Lay injunctions on women lightly for they are prisoners of the men and have no control over their persons.

> *4:34 Allah has made men superior to women because men spend their wealth to support them. Therefore, virtuous women are obedient, and they are to guard their unseen parts as Allah has guarded them. As for women whom you fear will rebel, admonish them first, and then send them to a separate bed, and then beat them. But if they are obedient after that, then do nothing further; surely Allah is exalted and great!*

M473 Feed and clothe your slaves well.

THE FINAL STATE OF CHRISTIANS AND JEWS

M453 When Mohammed first started preaching in Mecca, his religion was Arabian. Then Allah became identified with Jehovah and Jewish elements were introduced. When Mohammed moved to Medina, he argued with the Jews when they denied his status as a prophet in the Judaic line. He then annihilated the Jews and makes no more connections between Islam and the Jews. In his last statement, Jews and Christians became perpetual second class political citizens, *dhimmis* (pay the dhimmi tribute, *jizya*, and are subdued). Only those Christians and Jews who submit to Islam are protected. The real Christians are those who deny the Trinity and accept Mohammed as the final prophet. The real Jews are those who accept Mohammed as the final prophet. Both Christians and Jews must accept that the Koran is the true Scripture and that the Old Testament and New Testament are corrupt and in error. All other Jews and Christians are false and Kafirs.

> 9:29 *Make war on those who have received the Scriptures [Jews and Christians] but do not believe in Allah or in the Last Day. They do not forbid what Allah and His Messenger have forbidden. The Christians and Jews do not follow the religion of truth until they submit and pay the poll tax [jizya], and they are humiliated.*

A SUMMARY OF MOHAMMED'S ARMED EVENTS

I973 In a nine year period Mohammed personally attended twenty-seven raids. There were thirty-eight other battles and expeditions. This is a total of sixty-five armed events, and including assassinations and executions, for an average of one every six weeks.

MOHAMMED'S DEATH

I1000 When Mohammed spoke to Aisha, his favorite wife, she complained of a headache. Mohammed said, "No, Aisha, Oh my head. Would it distress you if you were to die before me so that I might wrap you in your shroud and pray over you?" Aisha said, "I think that if you did that, that after you returned to the house you would simply spend the night with one of your other wives." But the pain became worse and he took his final illness in the house of Aisha.

I1006 Mohammed weakened and was in a great deal of pain. Later he died with his head in Aisha's lap. His final words were the perfect summation of Islam, political action based upon religion.

> Bukhari4,52 288 *"There should not be two religions [no other religions besides Islam] in Arabia" and that the money should be continued to be paid to influence the foreign, Kafir ambassadors.*

T1831 Mohammed was buried beneath his bed. The bed was removed and a grave was dug where the bed had stood.

MOHAMMED AND SLAVERY

The term *slave* is a positive one in Islam. Mohammed referred to himself and Muslims as the slaves of Allah. Mohammed's second convert was a slave.

Mohammed himself was involved in every single aspect of slavery. He had non-believing men killed so their women and children could be made slaves[1]. He gave slaves away for gifts[2]. He owned many slaves, some of them black[3]. He passed around slaves to his companions for the purpose of sex, men who were his chief lieutenants[4]. He stood by while others beat slaves[5]. He shared the pleasure of forced sex with women slaves after conquest[6]. He captured slaves and wholesaled them to raise money for jihad[7]. One of his favorite sexual partners was a slave, who bore him a son[8]. He received slaves as gifts from other rulers[9]. The very pulpit he preached from was made by a slave[10]. He ate food prepared by slaves[11]. He was treated medically by a slave[12]. He had a slave tailor[13]. He declared that a slave who ran away from his master would not have his prayers answered[14]. And he approved an owner's having sex with his slaves[15].

This is the Sunna of Mohammed

---

1. A. Guillaume, *The Life of Muhammad* (London: Oxford University Press, 1982), 466.
2. Ibid., p. 499.
3. Ibid., p. 516.
4. Ibid., p. 593.
5. Ibid., p. 295.
6. Ibid., p. 496.
7. Ibid., p. 466.
8. William Muir, *The Life of Mohammed* (AMS Press, 1975), 425.
9. Ibid., p. 425.
10. Bukhari, Hadith, Volume 1, Book 8, Number 440.
11. Ibid., Volume 3, Book 34, Number 295.
12. Ibid., Volume 3, Book 36, Number 481.
13. Ibid., Volume 7, Book 65, Number 344.
14. Muslim, Hadith, Book 001, Number 0131.
15. Ibid., Book 008, Number 3383.

JEWS AND CHRISTIANS IN THE HADITH

CHAPTER 17

48:13 We have prepared a blazing Fire for these Kafirs
who do not believe in Allah and His Messenger.

AN INTRODUCTION TO THE HADITH

A hadith, or tradition, usually only a paragraph long, is an action, brief story, or conversation about or by Mohammed. A collection of these stories is called the Hadith or Traditions. So the Hadith is a collection of hadiths (the actual plural of hadith is ahadith).

The Hadith contains the Sunna (the ideal speech or action) of Mohammed, that is, his pronouncements. These hadiths are the very foundation of the Sharia, Islamic law.

These hadiths are sacred literature. For Islam, Mohammed is the model political leader, husband, warrior, philosopher, religious leader, and neighbor.

There are few hadiths about Christians since there were few in Arabia. Mohammed did not start attacking the Christians until the last year of his life.

HADITH

> Bukhari2,23,457 *While walking after dark, Mohammed heard a mournful cry and said, "Jews are being punished in the afterlife."*

Mohammed claimed the mantle of all the Jewish prophets. He claimed that Allah was Jehovah and that all religious truth came through Allah. Islam has the best claim to Moses.

> Bukhari3,31,222 *After coming to Medina, Mohammed witnessed the Jews observing a fast on the day of Ashura. Asked about that, they said, "This is holy day. It celebrates the day God delivered the Jews from their enemy. Moses fasted this day." Mohammed told them, "Muslims have more right to claim Moses as a prophet than you do." Consequently, Mohammed fasted that day and required all Muslims to fast that day.*

Bukhari4,56,662 *Mohammed said, "You will imitate the sinful behavior of your ancestors so utterly and completely that if they did something stupid, you would do exactly the same thing."*

We asked, "Are you talking about the Jews and the Christians?"

He answered, "Who else could I be talking about but the Jews and the Christians?"

Bukhari4,56,664 *Aisha despised the practice of praying with hands on the flanks because that was the way the Jews used to pray.*

Bukhari4,56,668 *Mohammed: "When the head of a Jew or a Christian becomes gray, they refuse to dye their hair. You must do the opposite of their behavior. Therefore, dye your hair and beard when they become gray."*

Jews are the cause of decay and rebellious wives.

Bukhari4,55,547 *Mohammed: "If it weren't for the Jews, meat would not rot. If not for Eve, wives would never disobey their mates."*

JEWS ARE FALSE; ISLAM IS THE TRUTH

Islam is pure and true. The Jews and their scriptures are corrupt and untrue, and the same is true of Christians and their scripture.

Bukhari3,48,850 *Ibn Abbas: "Muslims, why do you ask the Jews or Christians anything? The Koran, revealed directly to Mohammed, is the most-up-to date instruction that we have from Allah. You recite it word for word, and it is not modified. Allah tells you that the Jews and Christians have taken it upon themselves to change the word. They claim that their altered Scriptures are from God, but they make that boast to gain material rewards in this world. Hasn't enough been revealed to you through Mohammed to stop you from asking them anything? I never see any of them asking you about your revelations."*

Muslim037,6666 *Mohammed: "Allah will use a Christian or Jew to substitute for a Muslim in Hell."*

Some rats are changed Jews.

Muslim042,7135 *Mohammed: "A tribe of Bani Isra'il [Jews] disappeared. I do not know what became of them, but I think they mutated and became rats. Have you noticed that a rat won't drink camel's milk, but it will drink goat's milk?"*

The next hadith marks the beginning of religious apartheid in Arabia. To this day there are no churches, temples, or synagogues in Arabia.

> Bukhari3,39,531 *Umar drove the Christians and the Jews from Arabia. Mohammed defeated the Jews at Khaybar and gave ownership of the land to Allah, the Muslims, and Mohammed. But now Umar wished to evict the Jews. The Jews, however, asked to remain on the condition that they provide the labor to sustain the city and in return they would receive half of the proceeds. Mohammed said, "You may stay under those conditions until we change our minds." They remained in Arabia until Umar expelled them from the land.*

Jews are the enemy of Islam.

> Bukhari5,59,448 *During the battle of the Trench, Saed was badly wounded in the arm by an arrow shot by Hibban, a Quraysh. Mohammed erected a tent for Saed in the Mosque and visited him frequently. Pausing from the battle, Mohammed returned to his tent, removed his weapons and bathed. As he was shaking the dust from his hair, the Angel Gabriel revealed himself to Mohammed and said, "Have you quit the fight?"*
>
> *Mohammed said, "No."*
>
> *Gabriel replied, "Then attack them."*
>
> *Mohammed asked, "Where should I attack?"*
>
> *Gabriel pointed to the Jews. Mohammed then returned to battle and besieged the Jews who soon surrendered and put themselves in Mohammed's hands. Mohammed, however, gave the decision regarding their fate to Saed, who declared, "It is my judgment that their men be killed, their property confiscated, and their women and children enslaved."*
>
> *According to Hisham, his father told him that he heard Aisha say, "Saed said, 'Allah, you know that I love nothing more than to wage jihad against your enemies. I believe that you have now ended our struggle against the Quraysh. However, if there remains any fighting to be done between us, allow me to live and rejoin the fight against them. If, on the other hand, our battle with them has ended, let me die of my wounds right now. Blood immediately began to gush from the wound and streamed out of the tent, alarming those nearby."*

Two of the Jewish tribes of Medina had been exiled and their property taken. The above hadith marks the death knell of the remaining Jews. All the men were killed, the women made slaves, and the children were raised as Muslims.

Bukhari4,52,176 *Mohammed said, "You (Muslims) will fight with the Jews till some of them will hide behind stones. The stones will betray them saying, 'O 'Abdullah (i.e. slave of Allah)! There is a Jew hiding behind me; so kill him.' "*

KILL THE APOSTATE.

Bukhari9,89,271 *A certain Jew accepted Islam, but then reverted to his original faith. Muadh saw the man with Abu Musa and said, "What has this man done?"*

Abu Musa answered, "He accepted Islam, but then reverted to Judaism."

Muadh then said, "It is the verdict of Allah and Mohammed that he be put to death and I'm not going to sit down unless you kill him." [Death is the sentence for apostasy, leaving Islam.]

To be protected from Islam, Jews must submit to Islam.

Bukhari9,92,447 *We were at the Mosque one day when Mohammed came out and said, "Let's go talk to the Jews."*

When we arrived at their village, Mohammed addressed them saying, "Jews, submit to Allah. Become Muslim and you will be protected."

They answered, "You have delivered Allah's word, Mohammed."

Mohammed said, "That is my wish, accept Islam and you will be protected."

They repeated, "You have delivered Allah's word."

Mohammed said for a third time, "That is my wish; accept Islam and you will be protected," before adding, "You need to know that the Earth belongs to Allah, and I intend to expel you from this land. If you have property, you should sell it; otherwise, you had better remember that this land belongs to Allah and Mohammed."

Bukhari4,52,153 *Because the property of the Jews that Allah had given to Mohammed had not been won by the Muslims through the use of their horses and camels, it belonged exclusively to Mohammed. Mohammed used it to give his family their yearly allowance and he spent the rest on weapons and horses for jihad.*

THE DHIMMIS

CHAPTER 18

*5:92 Obey Allah, and obey the Messenger, and be on your
guard. If you do turn back, know that our Messenger
is only bound to deliver a plain announcement.*

Mohammed took his army a hundred miles from Medina to Khaybar and attacked the Jews. Islam was totally victorious. After taking the property of the Jews as the spoils of war, the Muslims made an agreement called a *dhimma* with them. The Jews could stay and farm the land if they gave Islam half their profits. They then became *dhimmis* who were under Sharia law.

Thus the word dhimmi came to mean permanent, second-class Kafir citizens in a country ruled by Islam. Dhimmis paid a special tax, and their civil and legal rights were greatly limited. The only way out of being a dhimmi was to convert to Islam or flee. The taxes from the dhimmis made Islam rich.

There are very few hadiths about dhimmis, but it was another of Mohammed's unique political inventions. The scorched-earth policy of killing all Kafirs was satisfying to the warrior, but it had an inherent problem. Once everyone was killed, the warrior had to find other work. Mohammed therefore created the policy of the dhimmi to deal with the Jews. Dhimmi status was expanded later to include Christians, Magians, and others.

Dual ethics is at the very core of the concept of a dhimmi. Political subjugation of Kafirs can only come about by viewing them as separate and apart from Allah's true human beings, Muslims.

The glory of Islam came not from Islam but its dhimmis' wealth and knowledge. The dhimmis were the scholars, since the Arabs of Mohammed's day were barely literate and whose classical literature was oral poetry. The secular knowledge of Islam came from the Christians, Persians, and Hindus.

Islam is credited with saving the knowledge of the Greeks from extinction. This is ironic in two ways. First, it was the jihad against the Byzantine/Greek culture that caused its collapse. Secondly, it was the

Syrian Christian dhimmis who translated all of the Greek philosophers into Arabic.

The Hindu numbering system was credited to Islam. The Muslims took the zero from Hindu mathematicians, and today we call our numbers Arabic numerals. From carpets to architecture, the Muslims took the ideas of the dhimmis and obtained historical credit. The lists of great Islamic scholars are mostly dhimmis with Arabic names living under Islamic dominance.

Over time, as the dhimmi population decreased, the "Golden Age" of Islam disappeared. There has never been a totally Islamic culture that was golden, brilliant or prosperous. Today there have only been eight Nobel prizes given to Muslims in the sciences. All of these prizes were given for work done with Kafirs in Kafir countries. There has never been a scientific Nobel prize given for work in a Muslim country.

Without the dhimmis, Islam is poor. The total economic output of all Arab countries (without the oil) is equal to that of Spain.

The dhimmis produced the wealth of Islam.

B4,53,388 Juwairiya said to Umar, "Oh, Caliph, give us your advice." Umar said, "You should continue the arrangement made by Mohammed regarding the dhimmis because the taxes they pay fund your children's future."

When Mohammed moved to Medina, half of Medina was Jewish. Less than two years later, two of the three tribes of Jews were exiled and their money and goods taken as spoils of war. The men of the third and last tribe were executed and their wives were taken as slaves of pleasure and domestic work; their children were raised as Muslims. Not one Jew was left in Medina.

After jihad comes dhimmitude: Jihad cracks open the culture; dhimmitude replaces it with Islam. Afghanistan was a Buddhist nation until conquered by Islam; Pakistan was Hindu; Egypt was the culture of the Pharaohs even though it had become Christian; and North Africa was Christian.

Today we locate cultures on continents, but up until 600 AD the Mediterranean Sea was the center of the map. Egypt was only a few days away from Italy, and Greek ships sailed into Egyptian harbors on a daily basis. Egypt and North Africa were much closer to the southern coast of the Mediterranean and European culture than they were African culture south of the Sahara. There was a Buddhist monastery in Alexandria, Egypt. The southern coast of the Mediterranean was once Roman, then became Christian. St. Augustine was from what is now called North Africa. Turkey was Christian and Buddhist. Iran (Persia) was Zoroastrian. The Hindu culture was twice as large as it is now.

Then came jihad, followed by dhimmi status. More than half of Christianity disappeared; half of Hindu culture disappeared; half of Buddhism was annihilated; Zoroastrianism disappeared. Languages were replaced by Arabic. The laws, customs, names, and history became extinct. When Napoleon invaded Egypt, he found that the Egyptian Arabs did not know anything about the pyramids or temples. Islam had annihilated even the memory of the pharaohs' 5,000-year-old culture.

So the progression was as follows: first jihad, then dhimmitude, and then the destruction of the native dhimmi culture. This became the model for the next 1400 years. The dhimmi became a second-class citizen in Islam and paid a heavy poll tax called the jizya. Only Jews and Christians and, sometimes, Magians (Zoroastrians) had the choice of becoming dhimmis. Buddhists, Hindus, and animists had the choice of death or conversion.

It was Umar II who set the standards for dhimmitude. His treaty with the dhimmis states:

> We shall not build, in our cities or in their neighborhood new monasteries, churches, convents, or monks' cells, nor shall we repair, by day or by night, such of them as fall in ruins or are situated in the quarters of the Muslims.
>
> We shall keep our gates wide open for passersby and travelers. We shall give board and lodging to all Muslims who pass our way for three days.
>
> We shall not give shelter in our churches or in our dwellings to any spy nor hide him from the Muslims.
>
> We shall not manifest our religion publicly nor convert anyone to it. We shall not prevent any of our kin from entering Islam if they wish it.
>
> We shall show respect toward the Muslims, and we shall rise from our seats when they wish to sit.
>
> We shall not seek to resemble the Muslims by imitating any of their garments.
>
> We shall not mount on saddles, nor shall we gird swords nor bear any kind of arms nor carry them on our persons.
>
> We shall not engrave Arabic inscriptions on our seals.
>
> We shall not sell fermented drinks.
>
> We shall clip the fronts of our heads (keep a short forelock as a sign of humiliation).
>
> We shall always dress in the same way wherever we may be, and we shall bind the zunar round our waists.
>
> We shall not display our crosses or our books in the roads or markets of the Muslims. We shall only use clappers in our churches very softly.

We shall not raise our voices when following our dead. We shall not take slaves who have been allotted to Muslims.

We shall not build houses higher than the houses of the Muslims.

Whoever strikes a Muslim with deliberate intent shall forfeit the protection of this pact.

(from Al-Turtushi, *Siraj Al-Muluk*, p. 229-30)

But this excerpt can not really describe the world of the dhimmi. Islam dominated all public space. The government was Islamic; the education was Islamic; dress was Islamic; literature was Islamic. Only inside the dhimmi's house could there be no Islam. The word of a dhimmi could not be used in court against a Muslim and crimes against dhimmis were rarely prosecuted.

The wealth of Islam came from the wealth and labor of the subjugated dhimmis. This had been true ever since Mohammed sent out his first jihadists to raid a Meccan caravan. From that day onward, Islam became wealthy through violence against the Kafir. The perfect example of the Jews of Khaybar as dhimmis was used again and again. First jihad took the spoils of war and slaves; then the dhimmi tax system produced yearly wealth. Islam is a political system with a divine license to take what is wanted from *dar al harb*, the land of war.

These rules created a dhimmi culture throughout sixty percent of what had been Christian and European culture. Dhimmitude resulted in the total loss of the local culture.

> 2:193 *Fight them until you are no longer persecuted and the religion of Allah reigns absolute, but if they give up, then only fight the evil-doers.*

The treaty of Umar ensured that this goal was met. The details of what happened varied from country to country. The Zoroastrian and Buddhist cultures collapsed under jihad and quickly disappeared. The Jews survived as the servants to Islam; some Christian cultures managed to exist for a thousand years before annihilation, and the Christians in other areas quickly became Muslims.

The actual attitude of Islam toward the dhimmis was more contempt than hatred, and over time the dhimmis disappeared. They either left or converted. It was too hard to be a second-class citizen, and the extra taxes were a burden. As time went on both Christians and Jews became more Arabic in their outlook; they started to treat women as the Arabs did and their customs became more and more Islamic. Finally it was easier to accept Islam as their religion and stop all the pressure and contempt.

HISTORY

Humiliation and contempt were an important part of the ethic in relating to Jews. The favorite epitaph for a Jew was the one Mohammed used, "apes." Christians were called "pigs." Dhimmis were never to have higher status than Muslims.

> QUESTION: *If a ruler prevents the dhimmis who live among the Muslims from building high and ornamented houses, riding horses inside the city, dressing themselves in sumptuous and costly garments, wearing kaftans with collars and fine muslin and furs and turbans, in sum from deliberate actions to belittle the Muslims and exalt themselves, will that ruler be rewarded and recompensed by God?*
>
> ANSWER: *Yes. The dhimmis must be distinguished from the Muslims by their dress, their mounts, their saddles, and their headgear.*[1]
>
> *And again:*
>
> *And whereas, in reply to this, my imperial decree had already previously been written and sent, concerning the dress of the infidels. Therefore I now command that when this present arrives, you proceed in accordance with my previously sent imperial decree and ensure that henceforth neither Jew nor Christian nor any other infidel be allowed to wear fine clothes, as set forth above, and in contravention of my previously issued noble command.*
>
> *(Given to the Inspector of Markets)*
> *15 August 1568.*[2]

And it was not wise for a Jew to enter into any theological discussions about Islam. Here is a comment about the Jews in Egypt by Edward Lane:

> At present, they are less oppressed; but still they scarcely ever dare to utter a word of abuse when reviled or beaten unjustly by the meanest Arab or Turk; for many a Jew has been put to death upon a false and malicious accusation of uttering disrespectful words against the Koran or the Prophet.[3]

This treatment was for all People of the Book, Jews and Christians. This scene is from Turkey in 1908:

---

1. Paul Horster, *Zur Anwendung des islamischen Rechts im 16. Jahrhundert* (Stuttgart, 1935), 37.

2. Ahmed Refik, *Onuncu asr-I hicride Istanbul hayati* (Istanbul, 1333), 68-9.

3. Edward William Lane, *An Account of the Manners and Customs of the Modern Egyptians*, 5th ed. (London, 1871), 305.

> *The attitude of the Moslems towards the Christians and Jews, to whom as stated above, they are in a majority of ten to one, is that of a master towards slaves whom he treats with a certain lordly tolerance so long as they keep their place. Any sign of pretension to equality is promptly repressed. It is often noticed in the street that almost any Christian submissively makes way even for a Moslem child. Only a few days ago the writer saw two respectable-looking, middle-aged Jews walking in a garden. A small Moslem boy, who could not have been more than eight years old, passed by and, as he did so, picked up a large stone and threw it at them—and then another—with the utmost nonchalance, just as a small boy elsewhere might aim at a dog or bird. The Jews stopped and avoided the aim, which was a good one, but made no further protest.[4]*

Islam could treat the dhimmi Jews and Christians in one of two ways, both equally acceptable. They could be physicians in the court of the caliph or they could be "apes" at which a small boy tossed a rock. Both roles are supported by the Koran of Mecca and the Koran of Medina, continuing the dualistic nature of Islam.

DHIMMITUDE

Today the formal status of dhimmi has been replaced by dhimmitude, the intellectual submission to Islam.

One of the marks of a dhimmi under the fourth caliph Umar was that a dhimmi was forbidden to study the Koran. The chief mark of dhimmitude today is ignorance of the Koran, the Sira and the Hadith. Dhimmitude only sees Islam in terms of Western values, political correctness and multiculturalism. An apologist for Islam is a dhimmi.

---

4   H.E. Wilkie Young, "Notes on the City of Mosul," enclosed with dispatch no. 4, Mosul, January 28, 1909, in F.O. 195/2308; published in Middle Eastern Studies 7 (1971): 232.

COMMENTS

CHAPTER 19

A SACRED TEXT

The doctrine described here is taken from Islam's foundational texts. The Koran and the Sunna of Mohammed are the basis of thought and action taken by Muslims against Christians and Jews.

What is so confusing is the contradictory nature of Islamic dualism. The early doctrine is favorable to Christians and Jews, but the later doctrine is about absolute political and religious domination over the People of the Book.

The more powerful Mohammed became, the more he increased the pressure against the Kafirs. This progression defines Islam's history with Christians and Jews. The doctrine is very pragmatic. When Islam is weak, be friendly. When Islam is strong enough, it exerts force and pressure as needed to subjugate the Kafirs.

The Golden Rule does not appear in any of Islam's texts.

JIHAD

For 13 years Mohammed preached the religion of Islam in Mecca and 150 Arabs joined. In Medina he turned to jihad and politics. Ten years after that every Arab submitted to Islam. The religion of Islam was a failure. Jihad and politics were a total success.

FIGURE 19.1: AMOUNT OF TRILOGY TEXT DEVOTED TO JIHAD

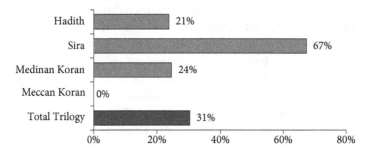

THE FALSE CHRISTIAN MUSLIM BOND

Go to any interfaith dialog and you will hear that Muslims, Jews and Christians are all part of the same "Abrahamic faith". Muslims will proudly say that they honor Jesus (called Isa in the Koran) and that Jesus is mentioned more times in the Koran than Mohammed. Islam, they imply, is just like Christianity and Judaism, but improved. Christians, Jews and Muslims are all "brothers in Abraham".

None of this is true.

Isa and Jesus

Jesus does not appear in the Koran, but a man named Isa is mentioned frequently (52 times). Is Isa the same as Jesus? Isa was born of the virgin birth with a mother named Mary. Isa is not the Son of God, but a prophet of Allah. Isa came to earth to predict the coming of Ahmed (Mohammed). Isa did not die, but was assumed bodily into Paradise. He was not crucified and he was not resurrected. Isa will return to kill the pig, break the cross, destroy churches and synagogs, end the *jizya* (the dhimmi tax), kill every Christian who does not believe in him, and establish Sharia law over all the world. He will marry and have a family. There will be 40 years of peace and then he will die to be buried at Medina.

Isa was not Jesus. Jesus was not Isa.

Abrahamic faith

The concept of an Abrahamic faith that is a common bond between Christians, Jews and Muslims is a favorite bridge building talk. If all three are of a common origin, they should have similar ethics.

Christianity and Judaism have a common ethic based upon the Golden Rule. Islam has no Golden Rule, but has dualistic ethics with one set of ethics for Muslims and another set of rules for Kafirs.

Christians accept the Hebrew Bible as being true. Islam says that both the Torah and the Gospels are corrupt and not fit for spiritual guidance.

Being of the same Abrahamic faith makes it difficult to explain the extensive Jew hatred in the Koran, Sira and Hadith. See the chart (next page). There is more Jew hatred in the Trilogy by both percentage and total content than in *Mein Kamph*. Where is the Abrahamic brotherhood?

Notice how the Jihad chart and the Anti-Jew chart both show the dualistic nature of Islam. Islam has one nature in Mecca and a contradictory nature in Medina. Even though they contradict, both are considered true doctrine.

FIGURE 19.2 ANTI-JEWISH TEXT IN TRILOGY

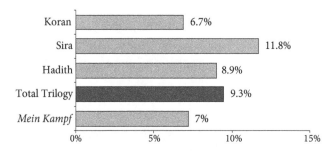

MOLESTATION OF THE MIND

Christians, Jews—Kafirs—accept violence and threats from Islam without protest. This acceptance of violence is the sign of a profoundly molested psyche.

Violent molestation can cause denial.

The Christians and Jews are classic manifestations of the abused wife and the abused child. The dhimmi is a broken person and doesn't even know it.

JEWS AS ISLAM'S MOLESTED CHILDREN

Mohammed murdered, enslaved, assassinated, tortured, and raped the Jews. He exiled them, took their wealth, and then made those remaining work the land that he stole from them. They also had to give him half of their profits. The Jews were the first dhimmis, semi-slaves.

Jews have developed amnesia about the Islamic destruction of the Jews in Arabia. The amnesia extends to life as a dhimmi under Islam. They were second-class citizens in Islam. Yet, many Jewish intellectuals are the chief apologists for Islam today.

When you read the current Islamic accounts of jihad, it is very clear that jihad is happening in Israel, Iraq, Kashmir, Sudan, the Philippines—but Jews don't see it that way. They have a "Palestinian problem," not jihad. Jews' profound ignorance about the doctrine and history of Islam does not allow them to think strategically. Islam has gelded Jewish intellectuals.

Jews are the abused children of Islam, they do not protest the insults of the Koran, Mohammed's brutality and their annihilation in Arabia. Today, Jews deny the Islamic roots of Jew hatred in Europe.

CHRISTIANS AS ISLAM'S MOLESTED CHILDREN

Political Islam used the sword to take over Syria, Egypt, North Africa, the Levant, and Turkey. Before jihad all of this territory was predominately Orthodox Christian. The victims could convert or become dhimmis. This is still going on today. Over 2,000,000 Christians were killed and enslaved in Sudan in the 20th century alone.

What has the rest of Christianity had to say about the slaughter of the Christians in the Middle East and other Islamic nations? *The great stain on Western Christianity is its denial of the suffering of its brothers and sisters in Christ at the hands of the Muslims.*

Christians are the abused children of Islam, due to their denial of suffering and their apologies for Islam.

THE ETHICS OF WILLFUL IGNORANCE

At this time the overwhelming majority of Christian and Jewish leaders know nothing about the doctrine of Islam. They do not speak of any criticisms about Islam in public, not even in their own houses of worship. Not only are they unable to speak the truth about Islam, they will not allow discussion about the topic.

Are these leaders afraid of a car bomb or an assassination? No, they are terrified of being called a bigot, an Islamophobe or intolerant. Ministers and rabbis see that the history of 1400 years of being dhimmis, the annihilation of Christianity, and Islamic slavery is never mentioned, never talked about.

In business law, there is a concept of willful ignorance, and it can be a felony. Should we not hold our religious leaders to a higher standard than a business leader?

In the light of Islam, all of our leaders are ignorant, but the religious leaders are the most disappointing.

FOR MORE INFORMATION

www.politicalislam.com
www.cspii.org
Facebook: @BillWarnerAuthor
Twitter: @politicalislam
YouTube: Political Islam

CPSIA information can be obtained
at www.ICGtesting.com
Printed in the USA
LVHW04s0510121018
593372LV00001B/78/P